The Illustrated Buddha for Beginners

The Illustrated Buddha for Beginners

Stephen T. Asma
AUTHOR & ILLUSTARTOR

JAICO PUBLISHING HOUSE
Ahmedabad Bangalore Chennai
Delhi Hyderabad Kolkata Mumbai

Published by Jaico Publishing House
A-2 Jash Chambers, 7-A Sir Phirozshah Mehta Road
Fort, Mumbai - 400 001
jaicopub@jaicobooks.com
www.jaicobooks.com

Published in arrangement with
Hampton Roads Publishing
65, Parker St. Unit 7
Newburyport, MA 01950, USA

To be sold only in India, Bangladesh, Bhutan,
Pakistan, Nepal, Sri Lanka and the Maldives.

THE ILLUSTRATED BUDDHA FOR BEGINNERS
ISBN 978-81-8495-880-5

First Jaico Impression: 2016

Printed by
Trinity Academy For Corporate Training Limited, Mumbai

Contents

Acknowledgments

First, in this and all things, my little Julien, and his mother, Wen.

Next, I wish to express my thanks to those who helped create and support this book, both in its earlier incarnation and its present manifestation. Many thanks to Jane Hagaman, Stacey Ruderman, and my old friend Peter Altenberg. Many years ago, Heidi Wagreich inspired much of the humor in this book and I remain grateful. I wish to acknowledge the fine folks at Hampton Roads Publishing, also my wonderful colleagues at Columbia College Chicago. Special thanks to my editor Greg Brandenburgh—a kindred goat, in a land of sheep. I am grateful to those friends, students, and teachers who understood that laughter is the proper response to sacrosanct dogma. Finally, this book is dedicated to my parents, Ed and Carol, who must be Bodhisattvas in disguise.

A New Introduction

This book first appeared in the late 1990s and found a substantial audience among the Buddha-curious, and even initiated Buddhist practitioners. Over the years it has been translated into Spanish, Hindi, and Chinese. I am proud to bring out this new revised edition with Hampton Roads Publishing, because it allows me to clarify further and nuance the basic arguments of the Buddha.

The original impetus for this book was the fact that Buddhism seemed deeply misunderstood in the West; unfortunately, that fact has not changed much. Unlike most other religious scriptures, which are comprised of parables, legends, and allegories, Buddhist teachings also contain actual philosophical arguments that were advanced by the Buddha himself. My little illustrated book is primarily about those arguments. I would accept a happy irony if my cartoon drawings lured people into those decidedly un-cartoonish philosophical arguments.

So skewed is the Western view of Buddhism that it will probably come as a surprise to many people that the Buddha gave rational arguments and empirical evidence in his teachings. Recently in one of my classes, an undergraduate student "informed me" that people in the East, like Buddhists, don't logically argue with each other—instead, they simply look at each other and read each other's minds with compassionate understanding. She had gathered this wisdom from American television shows, commercials, and movies, which proffer a cadre of mystical monk characters—usually helping some confused Westerner pick the right soda, or cell phone service, or some such consumer quandary. Stereotypes die hard, I know, and the tedium of consumer culture may always lead us to romanticize exotic monastic traditions. But it is my hope that this book will give searchers a little more grasp on the ethics, metaphysics, epistemology, and even logic of Buddhism.

Since this book first appeared, more than one person has asked me why my drawings of the Buddha look like Osama Bin Laden. I find this a little funny, but also a little disconcerting, since such a weird and unpleasant connotation hardly helps me make my case for Buddhism. I've had to assure readers that Bin Laden was not on my radar, nor anyone else's it would appear, when I first drew the Buddha several years before 9/11. The fact is that I first drew him modeled on myself, which I admit sounds like the height of narcissism—but as any illustrator knows, in the absence of a model, one has to rehearse facial expressions and body movements in a mirror. So Gautama, and many of the other characters, got rather exaggerated and modified versions of my own tired mug. No one really knows what the Buddha looked like, except to say that he had the ethnic features of a northern Indian. He was definitely not fat, nor did his features resemble those of Chinese or Japanese—and of course both those misrepresentations (fat and Far Eastern) are common. It is understandable that we should forget the Buddha's Indian origins, since Buddhism ceased to be prevalent in India about twelve hundred years ago, while it continued to dominate Asian cultures right up to the present.

Geographic prevalence explains the ethnic confusion, but why is he usually portrayed as fat? Two considerations may solve the mystery. First, we have to remember that in every other part of the world and at every other time in history, fat was a good thing to be. In our currently obese state of prosperity, Americans and the rest of the developed world are desperate to get thinner, but our historical predecessors had no such familiarity with empty-calorie bloating. Being fat was rare and it was a symbol of power, health, prosperity, and even social status. Being fat meant that your family had invested well in you, and that you in turn were probably a good spousal investment. Add to this the second consideration, that whenever Buddhism arrived in a new place, it did not arrive into a religious vacuum. As a religion, Buddhism had to compete in the marketplace of other traditions: in Tibet, Buddhism appeared as an interloper in a region dominated by the native animistic religion, Bon; in China, Buddhism seemed like an upstart next to Taoism and Confucianism; in Japan, Shinto was already dominant; and so on wherever the dharma traveled. A fat Buddha image may have been a powerful marketing tool in gaining converts in new lands.

This confusion, of the fat Chinese Buddha versus the skinny Indian Buddha, raises an important general distinction between the culture of Buddhism and the philosophy of Buddhism. Since first writing this book, I have traveled widely in the East, living for extended periods in Cambodia and China, but also spending time in Thailand, Laos, and Vietnam. It should come as no surprise that wherever I went, the Buddha statues in the temples looked remarkably like the locals. And the Buddhism itself looked almost like a different religion in the assorted countries. This is as it should be, because religions, like other cultural traditions, are supposed to help us with our local daily challenges. Buddhist rituals, for example, help people mourn the deaths of family members, celebrate weddings and births, bless new homes and businesses, and so on. Religious customs, then, are usually adapted to their unique social and even geographical environments. Within a single country like Cambodia, I found many different kinds of Buddhism.

Westerners who actually study Buddhism through books (and in some cases, even come to call themselves "Buddhists") are often shocked when they meet people from Buddhist countries who engage in elaborate rituals and beliefs—beliefs that look nothing like the Buddhism found in those Western books. At a Buddhist shrine in Vietnam, for example, I watched young couples offer six-packs of beer and piles of photocopied money to the altar, in hopes of securing an auspicious future wedding date. Or consider that in many Asian countries, more people know and love Guan Yin (a derivative Buddhist saint or Bodhisattva) than know about the historical Buddha Gautama. Or consider further the Western stereotype of Buddhism, as a strictly pacifistic, docile, and submissive style, compared to the mainstream views in many Asian countries of a powerful, ass-kicking, kung-fu version of Buddhism. In China, for example, Shaolin warriors are every bit as much a part of Buddhist culture as scrawny monks. And the famous Buddhist folk story, known all over Asia, of the monkey king (Sun Wukong) and his "Journey to the West" (Xi youji) is filled with a masculine Buddhism that few Westerners would recognize. It's tempting for us to say, "Oh, that cultural stuff isn't real Buddhism." But it is.

Philosophical Buddhism is the focus of this book, not because it's the real Buddhism, but because it's a seminal part of Buddhism (articulated by the man himself) and it's a part that currently lingers in obscurity. Roughly speaking, the philosophy of Buddhism can be found in the Four Noble Truths, and the corollary ideas of (a) the impermanence of all things, (b) the interdependence of all things, and (c) the doctrine of no self. When I point out, throughout this book, where Buddhist cultures or even later Buddhist schools conflict with the basic philosophical dharma, I do so not out of smugness but out of a sense of professional obligation—that's what philosophers do, they look for intellectual inconsistencies.

Ultimately, I believe in the philosophy of Buddhism, but I also love the cultures of Buddhism. I don't "believe" in it like a faithful person believes in a miracle; I believe in it because I've tested its psychological hypotheses, and I've analyzed its metaphysical commitments. To my mind, the benefit of Buddhism for everybody, East and West, has to do with its approach to retraining the human mind. If human beings could recalibrate the quick mental leap from impulse to craving to action, we might be able to avoid some of our usual forms of suffering: rage, humiliation, intoxication, addiction, and so on. Buddhism is an attempt to recalibrate that psychological tendency towards craving.

Buddhism is older than Christianity, older than Islam, deeper than the Ganges River and the Mekong. Today, more than five hundred million people worldwide practice Buddhism, and it manifests in many different forms. But whatever shape it takes, it always strives to free human beings from the life of suffering. It is a philosophy of emancipation. Like the river that swells after monsoon season and brings life to the parched land, Buddhism washes through the conscious mind—purifying, clarifying, and nourishing the psyche. The Buddha gives us an image to help us understand his message of liberation: the lotus flower. The lotus is rooted in the muck and mire of the muddy riverbed, but it rises up and out of the water, ultimately flowering in the clear open air. Human beings are rooted in the chaotic world of desires, but with discipline they are capable of rising above their desires and attaining nirvana, even while they remain connected to this physical world. Buddhism is not an otherworldly philosophy. It is a path for better living in this impermanent world. According to the Buddha, it is not really possible for me to control the external course of things (which is the strategy of most other devotional religions), but if I can control my own internal mind, then there is no need to control the external world.

CHAPTER I

The Quest of the Young Prince

Just as there are many forms of Christianity in the West, so too there are many different manifestations of Buddhism in the East. And just as there was supposedly one Jesus who lived and taught in Galilee almost two thousand years ago, so again was there one historically real man who walked the northern Indian landscape and became the "Buddha" (Enlightened One). His name was Siddhartha Gautama and this book is primarily concerned with introducing him and his teachings rather than the whole spectrum of later Buddhist developments.

The West becomes enchanted with Buddhism in what seem like cycles of searching spiritualism. In the nineteenth century, American and Continental Transcendentalists recognized the wisdom of Buddhism and sought to deal with it in some fashion. In the "Beat" era of the twentieth century, every bongo-playing poet had a copy of Buddhist scriptures in his pocket.

And lamentably, in this day of the "New Age," every occult thing from "crystal healing" to psychic spoon-bending is spuriously linked with Buddhism or "Eastern spirituality." Thankfully, the historical Buddha was not as silly as the recent superstitions that illegitimately intone his name.

Gautama was born in the Ganges Valley near Gorakhpur between Nepal to the north and the Indian city of Varanasi (Benares) to the south. Many scholars maintain that Lumbini, just inside the modern Nepalese border, is his true birthplace.

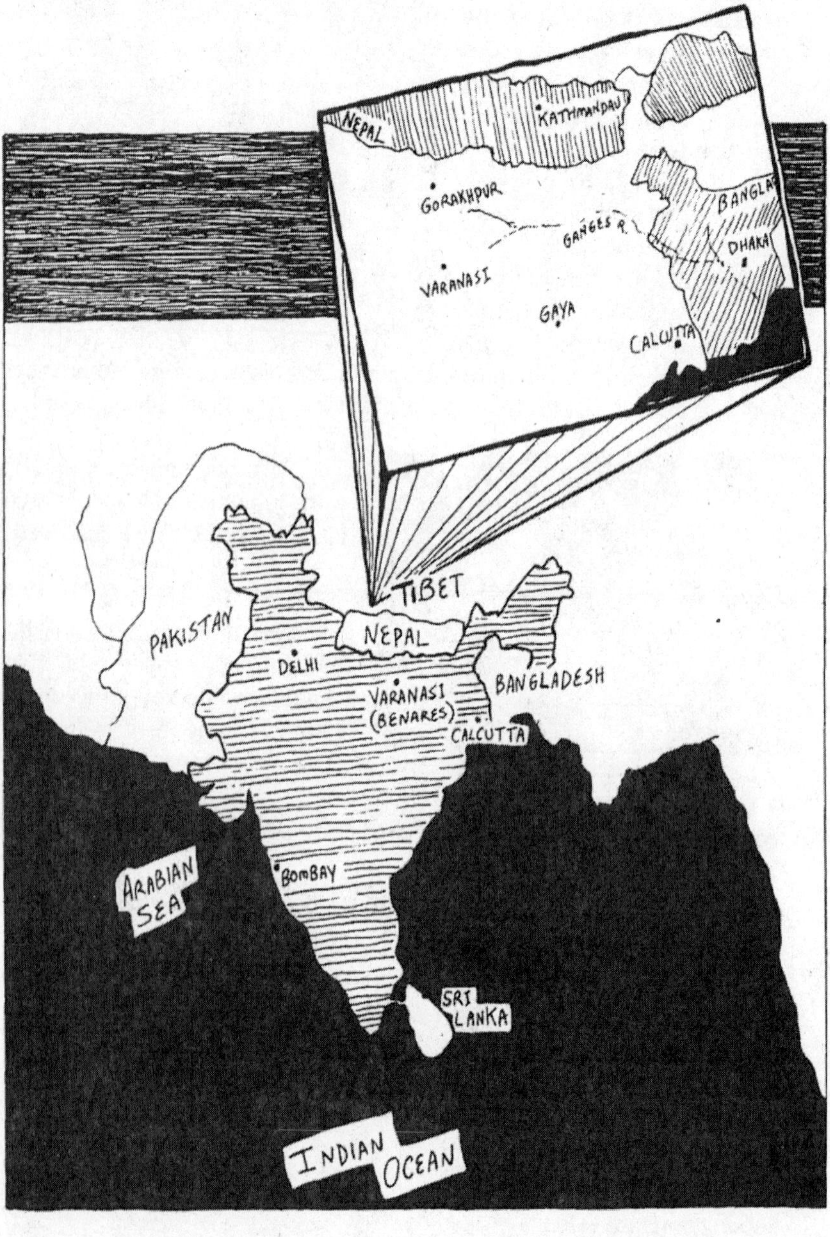

He was born in 563 BCE to king Suddhodana and his wife Maya (both from the tribe of Shakyas), and legend has it that when he was born, a "seer" foretold that he would one day leave his family to wander as an ascetic holy man. Suddhodana feared that the prophesy might come to pass and, after Maya's early death, he and Gautama's Aunt Prajapati sought to shelter the boy from the world outside the palace. Lest Gautama be lured away, the overprotective father and aunt surrounded the young prince with every kind of luxury and sought to insulate him from any images of suffering.

Being a prince and enjoying the benefits of such a station, Gautama undoubtedly received a fine education and, of course, a share of Brahmanic spiritual tutoring in the Upanishads and Vedic Hindu scriptures—but perhaps not too much spiritual tutoring since Suddhodana hoped for the kind of pragmatic and commonsensical heir that might one day succeed his rule.

Eventually, Gautama married his cousin Yosodhara and they had a son named Rahula.

The family lived peacefully and pleasurably, but in a state of happy ignorance about the world at large.

In time, however, the prince glimpsed the suffering and death of human beings beyond the palace walls, and this new awareness awakened a compassion for his fellow human beings and a distaste for his current sheltered privilege. Gautama's increasing concern with the suffering of human beings is crystallized in a legendary episode wherein he experiences for the first time an elderly and decrepit man, then a maimed individual . . .

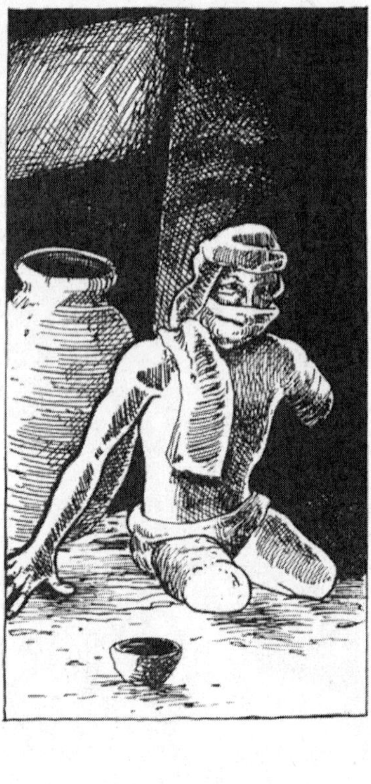

. . . and finally a corpse.
These sights are relatively new to the young man and he is further disturbed when he is informed that such is the fate of all human beings.

Though sources regarding Gautama's family life are scant, we have every reason to believe that he was a loving husband and father. Somewhere in the back of his mind, however, was a restless sense of incompleteness and an increasingly overpowering empathy for less fortunate people. How could he remain in his artificial bliss, he thought, when the world around him was suffering? And how could he continue to ignore the brute fact that his beloved wife and son would one day wither into suffering infirmity and death?

With the goal of discovering the truth about life and death, Gautama resolved to leave behind his home and family and to return only after he had procured the antidote. Late one night, when he was twenty-nine years old, Gautama gazed long upon his sleeping wife and child and then quietly departed from the palace. Thus did he relinquish everything he had known and loved up to that point in his life.

It is an interesting paradox that in order for Gautama to become enlightened and cure the puzzle of human suffering, he had to cause more of it by leaving his family.

In order to understand the course of Guatama's spiritual journey, it is important to appreciate the philosophical and religious context of India at the time. The Hindu system of beliefs is very diverse, but their common roots are in the ancient scriptures known as the Upanishads (circa 900–200 BCE) and the older Vedas (dating as far back as 1200 BCE).

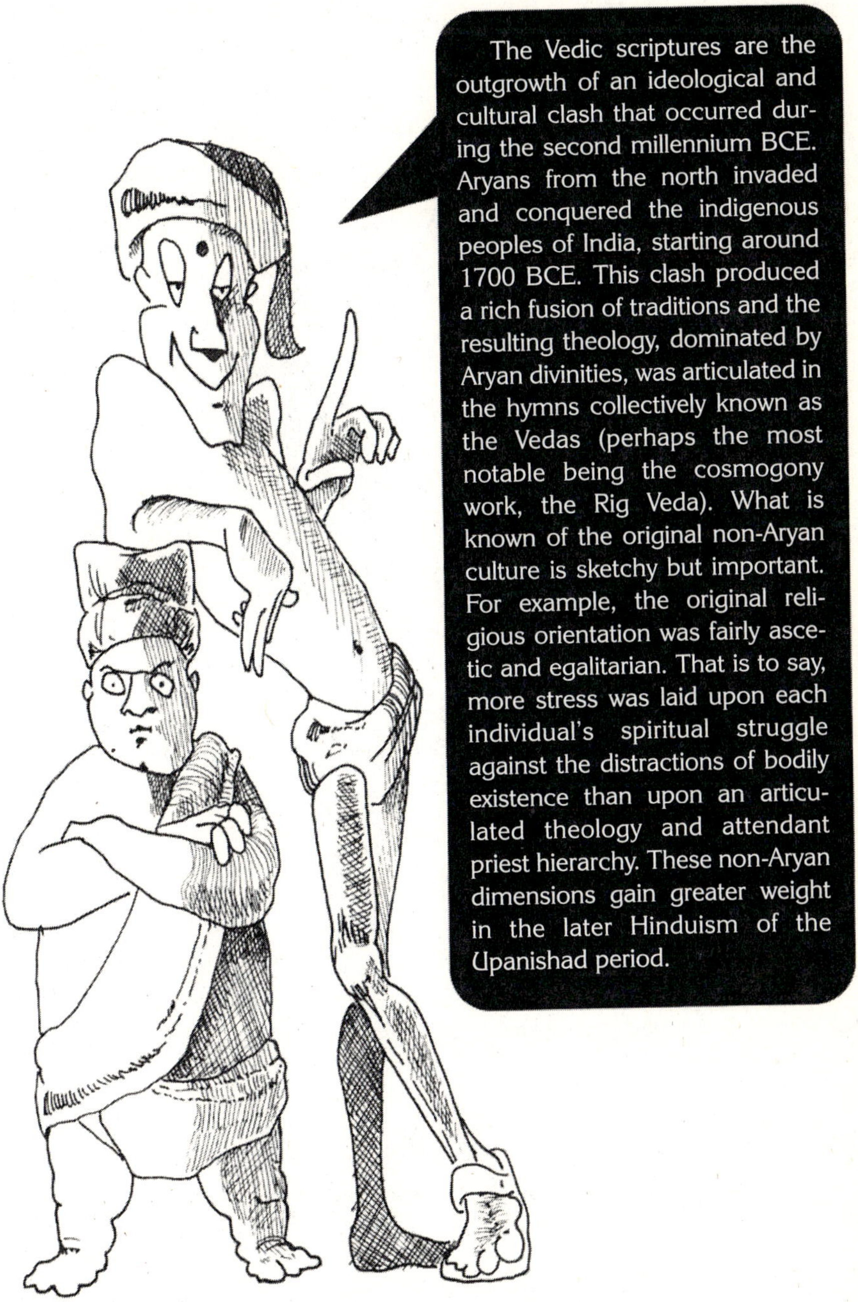
The Vedic scriptures are the outgrowth of an ideological and cultural clash that occurred during the second millennium BCE. Aryans from the north invaded and conquered the indigenous peoples of India, starting around 1700 BCE. This clash produced a rich fusion of traditions and the resulting theology, dominated by Aryan divinities, was articulated in the hymns collectively known as the Vedas (perhaps the most notable being the cosmogony work, the Rig Veda). What is known of the original non-Aryan culture is sketchy but important. For example, the original religious orientation was fairly ascetic and egalitarian. That is to say, more stress was laid upon each individual's spiritual struggle against the distractions of bodily existence than upon an articulated theology and attendant priest hierarchy. These non-Aryan dimensions gain greater weight in the later Hinduism of the Upanishad period.

The Vedic literature develops the basic pantheon of Hinduism. A trinity of gods—Brahma, Vishnu, and Shiva—forms the hub of Hindu beliefs.

Brahma is a kind of nonpersonal first principle for all creation, while Vishnu (the preserver) and Shiva (the destroyer) are subjects of many mythologies. Vishnu is the cosmic principle that holds reality in existence, while Shiva transforms reality into novel forms by bringing about destruction. The three deities are religious manifestations of the endless natural cycles of generation and corruption, birth and death. Later Hindu texts (after the death of Buddha), the Bhagavad Gita and Ramayana, continue the theology of Vishnu in different incarnations—Krishna and Rama, respectively.

SHIVA
How 'bout cuttin' me some slack, big guy?

In the time of Gautama, the Vedic traditions had grown increasingly ritualistic, and a class of priests, known as Brahmins, had developed into the established peddlers of religious truth.

The Vedic tradition embraced an "anatomical" metaphor for a sanctified social order or caste system. The Brahmin or priest class represented the "head" of an organism; the warrior and the class of nobility represented the "arms"; the merchant and craft class represented the "thighs"; and the peasant class represented the "feet." It was imperative, according to Hindu thought, that individuals of each caste resign themselves to their respective stations in the cosmic order.

We know that Gautama became rather hostile towards the priest class and eventually preached against the common practices of ritual animal sacrifice and hollow ceremony. Gautama's social status cannot be entirely irrelevant to this issue as well, for there was a strong emphasis in the Upanishad literature, written in the centuries before and during Gautama's life, upon the warrior and princely class (Ksatriya) to which Gautama belonged. This emphasis indicates the general devaluation of the Brahmin class from their previous privilege, and it may give insight into the Buddha's eventual healthy distrust of authority.

The impact of the Upanishads upon Hinduism was to revitalize the pre-Aryan dimensions of the culture. The Aryan culture was more worldly than ascetic; their religious ceremonies, for example, exalted the use of intoxicants (soma) and stressed the power of sacrifice and prayer to manipulate the gods. But the idea that the gods could be bribed for gifts and intoned as curses upon enemies came to be challenged by the rationalism of some of the Upanishad writings, and the Buddha's eventual claim that human beings "save" themselves ultimately completed this rejection of prayerful groveling and sacrificial bargaining.

Brahmin rituals increasingly became vehicles by which people could seek earthly benefits.

In addition to the distrust of priestly authority, the Upanishads reintroduced (probably from pre-Aryan times) an important non-Vedic doctrine into Hinduism: reincarnation or transmigration. Transmigration (samsara) is the idea that after death, one is reborn into a new physical body and life continues on. The laws that dictate what kind of rebirth one might expect are summarized as "karma" (consequences of actions).

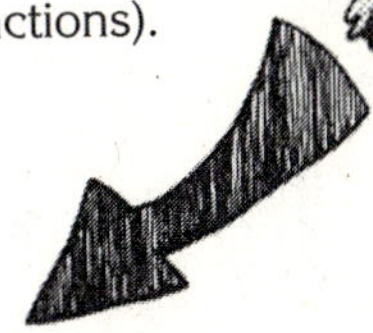

Samsara and karma are basic principles of Hinduism, and as such the historical Buddha was more than familiar with them.

When Gautama left his home and family, he first sought spiritual guidance from a famous Brahmin named Arada Kalama. Arada taught that the self or "atman" was an eternal soul that one could eventually release, over many lifetimes, from the bondage of material existence. Apparently, the Buddha was unimpressed with the teachings of Arada and sought further instruction under the guru Udraka Ramaputra.

Udraka also taught that belief in an underlying spiritual "self" or soul was crucial to a healthy moral pathway. It was this underlying immaterial self that transmigrated after death, and if karma determined one's future life, then one would act morally upright now in order to protect one's self down the road. But again Gautama was unimpressed with this doctrine of a transmigrating substantial soul and left the Brahmins to search elsewhere.

The Jains were an offshoot of mainstream Hinduism, distinctly heterodox in the sense that they basically ignored the Vedas and the Brahmins who interpreted them. They embraced the doctrine of karma and the dualistic metaphysics of matter and spirit, but they moved away from ritual and scholarly religion in favor of moral action. Actually, for the Jain, the highest moral action is no action at all. This is because all life is a relation between souls and matter, and it is matter that is ruled by chains of karmic causality. To act at all, say you cook up a steak for dinner, is to set in motion some chain of events that will come back at you and thereby keep you in the game of material life. According to the Jain, the killing and eating of this animal has created a causal chain of pain that will inexorably lead back to its originator. In this way, one's spiritual self cannot get free of one's material (karma-determined) self. The solution to this predicament, according to Jainism, is to act as little as possible; only in this way will one be released from the cycles of causality and pain. The lifestyle of the Jain is monastic and incredibly austere. Only through austere non-action can one annihilate karmic matter and thereby allow the soul to rise to its natural state of tranquil bliss.

Gautama adopted this ascetic lifestyle and through self-denial and non-action he sought to learn the truth about the human condition. Like other extreme ascetics, he probably filtered his drinking water to avoid accidentally ingesting and killing small life forms; he may have worn a breathing mask to stop the inadvertent breathing of insects; he walked carefully to avoid stepping on a life; and he starved himself as a negation of the bodily drives that lead to karmic imprisonment. The ultimate goal of this life is to have the self-control and discipline to simply fast oneself to death.

A contemporary of Gautama's was the Jain sage Vardhamana (Mahavira) who actually accomplished this ideal of death through fasting and thereby achieved the ultimate goal of non-injury (ahimsa). The Jains who followed Vardhamana, called the Digambaras ("sky-clad"), wore no clothing, as a symbol of their detachment from worldly conventions, and were often depicted with plant vines scaling around them because they had not moved for so long from their meditation.

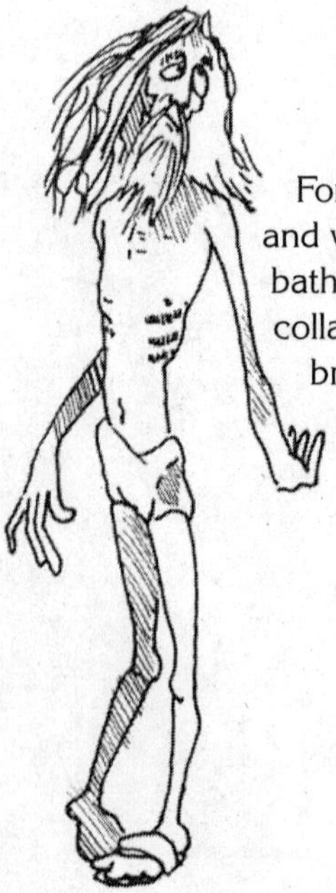

For six years Gautama practiced ascetic self-denial and withered to a walking corpse. One day, while bathing in the river, his strength failed him and he collapsed into the water. If not for an overhanging branch, Gautama would have drowned from his inability to overcome the gentle current.

After regaining the shore, he collapsed and lay suffering until a young woman named Sujata discovered him and returned with nourishment.

On that day Gautama realized that his life of austerity had revealed no deep truths to his searching mind; in fact, the starvation and dehydration had only distracted and diverted him from spiritual understanding. He vowed to lay down the life of extreme asceticism and henceforth to nourish the body as a part of the true path. The life of self-negation was as extreme and unproductive as his previous life of incessant luxury.

Finally, Gautama came to a tree and resolved to sit beneath it and meditate his way to perfect truth. Using his own meditation technique of mindfulness (sati), Gautama fell into a deep trance state. After many hours he was able to detach from his senses, his emotions, and his desires. Next he entered a state of pure inner consciousness and awareness, and ultimately a nonconscious ecstasy. In that ecstasy, he grasped the elusive cause of suffering, the pathway around suffering, and the nature of supreme peace (nirvana). That day Gautama became the Buddha (the enlightened one).

The Buddha went on to share his insights, gathering large numbers of disciples throughout the Varanasi area. He taught them the dharma, the path or system of correct living that would free them from suffering (dukkha). He argued that enlightenment was available to everyone. Neither a priest class nor a transcendent God bestowed truth upon the searcher. Attaining nirvana is ultimately within the power of all human beings; human beings save themselves through the highly disciplined path that Gautama first discovered. Subsequently, it is not the Buddha himself that is of paramount importance; rather, it is the path itself.

What, exactly, is the Buddha's philosophy?

CHAPTER II

The Wheel of Becoming

The relationship between the Buddha's philosophy and Hinduism is complex. When the traditional mythology of the Vedas was examined and developed in the Upanishads, Indian philosophy became focused upon the nature of Brahman (God as "first cause"). And more important, Hindu thinkers attempted to articulate the relationship between Brahman and each individual person's soul or self—in Sanskrit, "atman." Are we, as individual persons, related to the Godhead in some way?

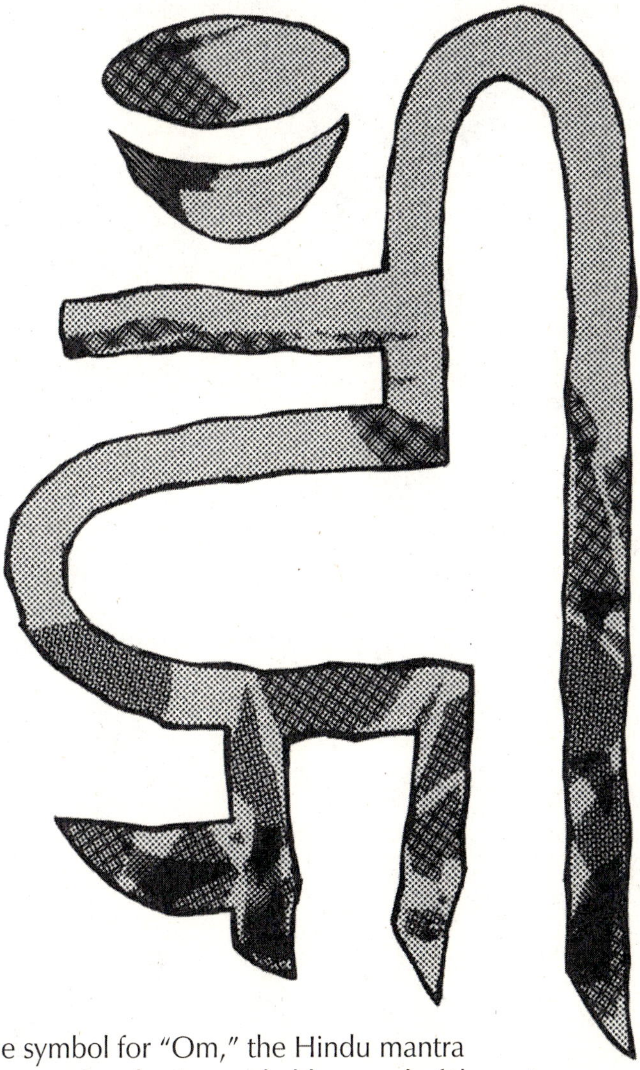

The symbol for "Om," the Hindu mantra representing the imperishable sound of the universe

Unlike the Judeo-Christian God, Brahman has no anthropomorphic personality.
NAUGHTY/NICE

God, in the Upanishads, is the creative originating principle for the entire cosmos. All of nature is in a relentless state of flux or becoming. Animals grow old and perish, seasons come and go, political empires pass away, solar systems arise and collapse . . .

. . . and bell-bottoms go in and out of fashion. All these things make up the ever-changing world of "Becoming," but these are really only manifestations of the all-encompassing reality.

The all-encompassing foundation is Being itself or Brahman, which is the source of all created things. Underlying all the changes of the natural world lies the changeless essential reality of God.

The relationship between Brahman and Nature is different from the Western conception. Most Western theologians (with some few exceptions, such as Spinoza) picture God as "outside" the cosmos, transcending above and beyond His created object (the universe). Like a skilled watchmaker who stands apart from her created timepiece, God stands apart from the created cosmos. In the West, God might occasionally step into the mundane realm to wind His clock—perhaps making a statue or two weep miraculously—but generally speaking, the Deity is unsullied by the material world.

In the Hindu tradition, however, God is not only the antecedent and transcendent world-maker, Brahman is also the world itself. The natural world around us that we encounter on a daily basis is not simply God's created artifact—it is Brahman itself. The natural world is just a manifestation of God and the two cannot really be separated.

In the Chandogya Upanishad (chapter 6), the novice Svetaketu asks his sage father, Aruni, how God can be present everywhere and yet go undetected by the senses. Aruni demonstrates with an analogy.
"Place this salt in the water and come to me in the morning."
"That salt you placed in the water last evening, please bring it here."
He looked for the salt but could not find it because it had completely dissolved.
"Please take a sip of it from this end. How is it?"
"Salt."
"Take a sip from the middle. How is it?"
"Salt."
"Take a sip from the other end. How is it?"
"Salt!"
It is always the same.
Like the salt that infuses all of the water but remains unseen, so too Brahman is the omnipresent yet invisible principle of reality.
"Verily, indeed, my dear, you do not perceive Pure Being here. Verily, indeed, it is here."

More important for understanding the Buddha's philosophical revolution is the related Hindu concept of atman or "soul." Just as there is this permanent essential reality underlying Nature called Being or Brahman, there is also an unchanging permanent dimension of human beings—namely, atman. The principal lesson of the Upanishads is that both the fluctuating cosmos and the ever-changing material human body are only distracting veils (maya) over the important spiritual reality. In the case of human beings, there is a changeless soul or "ego" that provides the continuity beneath the fleeting material person.

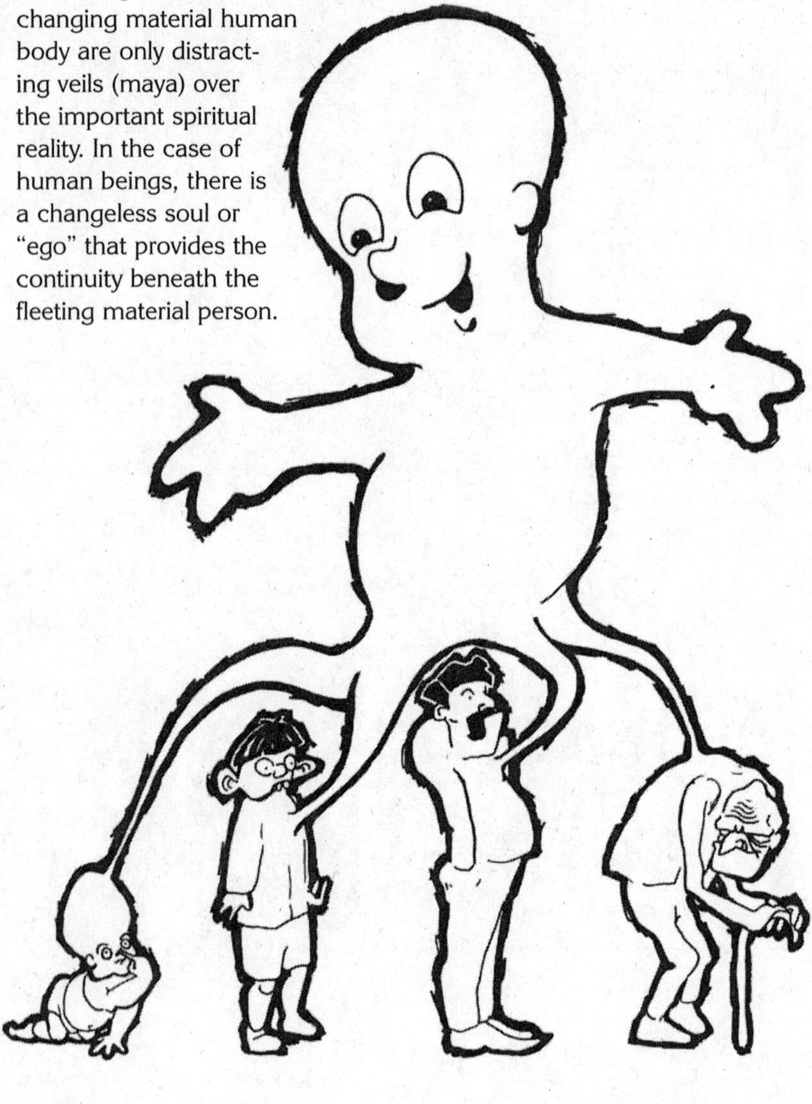

Atman, though unseen and unheard, is the "ruling" part of the individual creature. It is this subtle essence—this immutable core self—that makes up the true self. And in a famous phrase from the Upanishads, the sage Aruni repeatedly explains the atman to Svetaketu and proclaims "That art thou" (tat tvam asi).

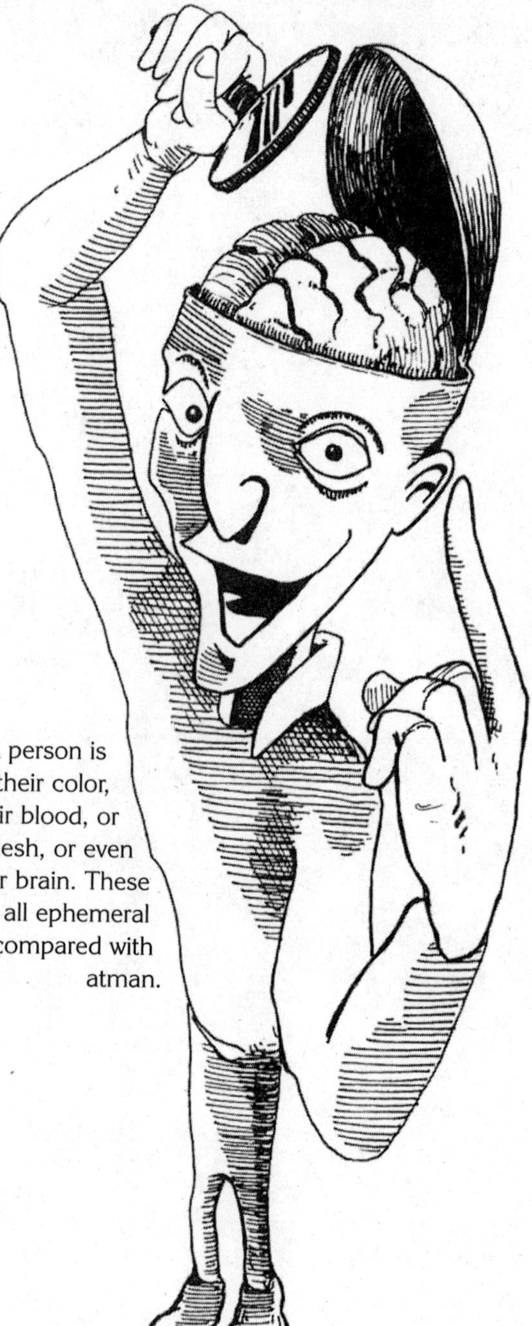

A person is
not their color,
or their blood, or
their flesh, or even
their brain. These
are all ephemeral
compared with
atman.

In other words, according to Hindu philosophy, one shouldn't get hung up on the trivial trials and tribulations of one's daily life, for all of it will pass. But the core self will always remain through this life and the next and the next.

It is the self or ego that migrates from one body and lifetime to another. Karma is both produced (kartr) and received (bhoktr) throughout different life spans by this eternal self—it is the "agent" and "patient" of karma. Much like the Western concept of an afterlife, there is something psychologically soothing about the idea that one's essential self will live beyond this lifetime.

The last, and perhaps most difficult, part of Hindu philosophy for us to understand is the relationship between Brahman and atman. Brahman is God and atman is the individual self, but in a deeper sense they are both the same thing.
Say what?
Most properly speaking, there is only one permanent reality and that is God, but the individual selves are manifestations or expressions of God temporarily separated from itself. There is an ideal unity of the soul of the human (atman) and the soul of the universe (Brahman). Individual selves are related to God like sparks to a fire . . .
. . . or water droplets to the sea—they are not qualitatively different and yet they are temporarily estranged from each other.
So why does God break itself up into individual egos? What's the point of it all?

The transcendent unmanifested Brahman does not need to achieve liberation from ignorance, because it is already completely perfected and free. But the eternally Divine God seeks to express itself through many conscious selves because in this way it is able to rise above ignorance. As the cosmic play unfolds, human egos continue to conquer the challenges of living and realize self-knowledge. With this conquering of ignorance, we are reunited with the Universal Consciousness and this saga is one of the infinite expressions that flow from Brahman.

The aim of the
Cosmic Dance
is to celebrate itself.

Having explored the basic metaphysics of Hindu philosophy, we can better understand both the similarities with and the radical differences from Buddha's teachings. The most shocking break from previous thinking is the Buddha's rejection of the concept of "self."

One of the central, and least understood, concepts of the Buddha's philosophy is the doctrine of "no-self" (anatman). The Hindu philosophy correctly pointed out the impermanent nature of the human body, the fallibility of the senses, and the fleeting character of daily consciousness. But despite all this flux and alteration, an inner agent, atman, persisted. The Buddha embraced this theory of the impermanence of all things but pushed the theory further than the Upanishads and claimed that this supposedly permanent self, atman, was itself a fiction. Just as the Upanishad philosophers reprimanded people for thinking that the changing material world was reality, the Buddha now reprimanded the Upanishad philosophers for thinking that the self was reality.

To argue that there is no immortal self is to pull a very comforting rug out from under religious thinking. The idea that some part of us lives on and on is pleasing and satisfies our craving for immortality. According to the Buddha, however, satisfying cravings is not the path to truth.

Not only is there no evidence for an immortal self, but to believe in its existence, according to the Buddha, will lead to an immoral life. It leads to evil because such a belief is ultimately ego-centered and selfish, and human beings will be unable to free themselves if they are seeking rewards in their future lives.

In the Samyutta Nikaya, the Buddha states:

"All formations are transient; all formations are subject to suffering; all things are without self [anatman]. Form is transient, feeling is transient, mental formations are transient, consciousness is transient."

According to the Buddha, realizing and understanding that we have no immortal self or soul is part of the enlightenment process—it is a feature of our awakening:

"Suppose, a man, who can see, were to behold the many bubbles on the Ganges as they are driving along. And he should watch them and carefully examine them. After carefully examining them, they will appear to him as empty, unreal, and unsubstantial.

"In exactly the same way does the monk behold all the bodily forms, feelings, perceptions, mental formations, and states of consciousness—whether they be of the past, or the present, or the future, far or near. And he watches them and examines them carefully, and, after carefully examining them, they appear to him as empty, void, and without a self" (chapter 22).

The Buddha rejects the idea of a substantial self that migrates from body to body; there is nothing like an immaterial soul (whether it be Christian, Hindu, or Platonic) that can exist independently of body. In the Majjhima Nikaya, Buddha states: "It is impossible that anyone can explain the passing out of one existence and the entering into a new existence . . . independent of bodily form, feeling, perception, and mental formation" (chapter 28). The immaterial self is an unverifiable fiction.

In the Potthapada sutra, the Buddha argues that a man who busies himself with souls is like a man who is madly in love with a woman whom he has never seen, or otherwise experienced, and about whom he knows absolutely nothing. In other words, it's a mind game.

In the Brhadaranyaka Upanishad (Book 2, chapter 4), the self is said to underlie the veneer of daily life: "Not for the sake of the husband is the husband loved, but for the sake of the self is the husband loved. Not for the sake of the wife is the wife loved, but for the sake of the self is the wife loved. Not for the sake of the sons are the sons loved, but for the sake of the self are the sons loved."

But the Buddha points out that invoking the self in this way really adds nothing to our understanding; nothing is added by positing a self behind every thought or feeling.

In the Majjhima Nikaya, Buddha states: "If there really existed the Ego, there would be also something that belonged to the Ego. As, however, in truth and reality, neither an Ego nor anything belonging to an Ego can be found, is it therefore not really an utter fool's doctrine to say: This is the world, this am I; after death I shall be permanent, persisting and eternal?" (chapter 22)

But far more shocking than the idea that no substantial self exists between lives is the Buddha's claim that neither does a substantial self exist within a lifetime.

The ego that ties together all of one's perceptions and feelings and thoughts is figmentary, according to the Buddha. Contrary to the model of Descartes, we cannot deduce the existence of an "I" from the act of thinking (cogitating). A person is really only a bundle of perceptions.

There is nothing "substantially" the same in my childhood and adulthood, but the causal process itself gives a kind of continuity between bundles of thoughts and impressions.

The Buddha dispels the myth of the metaphysical self (atman) as an underlying entity through life spans and between life spans. But he understands that each person feels a sense of her or himself as a self or ego. This palpable experience of the "I" is not completely illusory, for the Buddha claims that it is produced out of the combinations or conjunctions of feeling (vedana), perception (sanna), disposition (sankhara), consciousness (vinnana), and body (rupa). These are the five aggregates (khanda) or bundles of personhood and though each of these is impermanent and always fluctuating, they combine into the "felt" sense of the personal ego.

Interestingly enough, the Buddha did not turn to a purely materialistic philosophy after he decried the existence of atman. There was a school of Indian philosophy prior to the Buddha, founded by Carvaka (date unknown), which held that all knowledge came exclusively from the senses (like the Greek sophist Protagoras) and all reality was comprised exclusively of the material elements.

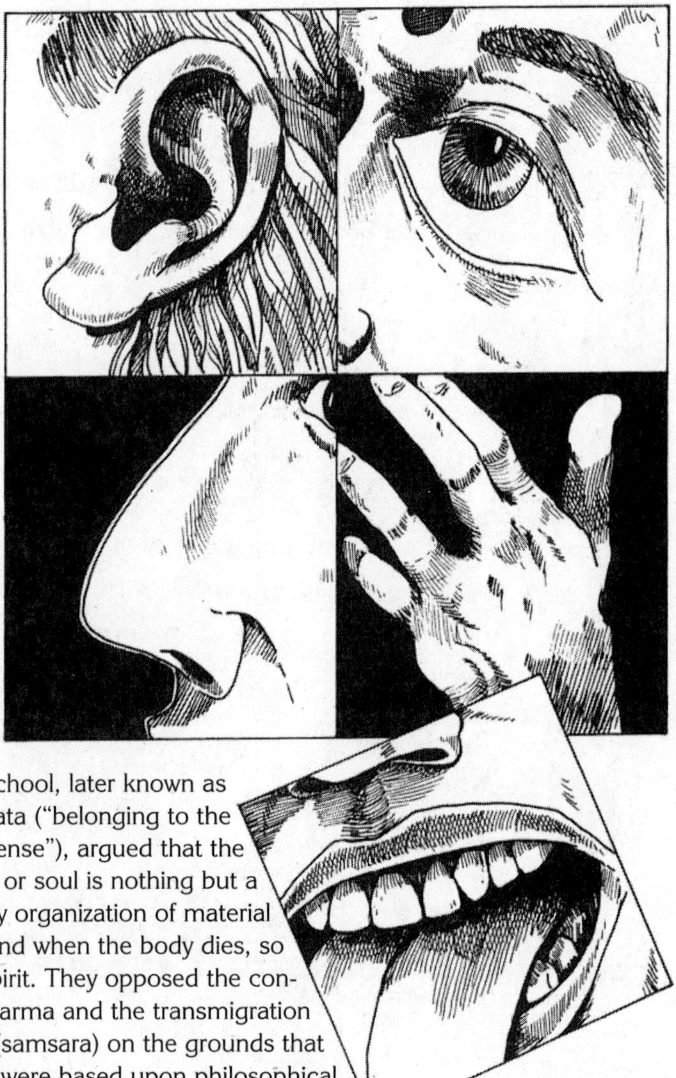

This school, later known as Lokayata ("belonging to the world of sense"), argued that the spirit or soul is nothing but a momentary organization of material elements and when the body dies, so too the spirit. They opposed the concept of karma and the transmigration of souls (samsara) on the grounds that these were based upon philosophical inferences rather than sense perceptions.

All the rituals and teachings of the Brahmins were considered to be the work of charlatans, and the Lokayata supposedly gave themselves over to the life of sensual gratification. The cause and effect of the material world impinging upon our perception was considered to be the final word concerning the nature of existence.

Though the Buddha did reject the reality of "self," there are two important reasons why this did not lead him to a purely materialistic philosophy. The first point, which I discuss in detail in the next chapter, is that the Buddha's entire conception of freedom is to break away from causality itself. Gratification of the senses, as the materialists recommended, is the sure path to attachment and slavery.

Second, the Buddha, in rejecting atman, never rejected the truth of karma or rebirth. Although it is true that a higher moral law (karma) is not something sensed in the normal way (seeing, hearing, smelling, touching, and tasting), its truth was not just an inference for the Buddha. Materialists dismissed karma on the grounds that it could not be experienced through the senses, but the Buddha's intensive yogic training allowed him to intuit or perceive truths in meditation without the traditional five senses. The Buddha developed a sixth sense, as it were, which allowed him to see the reality of karma and transmigration; he "perceived" rather than "conceived" the wheel of becoming. This might be akin to the saints of the West actually "seeing" or "feeling" God (revealed theology) rather than "arguing" for Its existence (natural theology).

This is where Buddhism becomes extremely difficult to grasp, for if there is no substantial self, then what exactly transmigrates? What exactly is the subject and object of karma? If there is no self, then how can I go on to a next life and be held responsible for actions in this life? Indeed, if I am not the person I was a year ago or even two days ago, then how can praise or blame concerning past actions be fixed to me—for I am no longer that person who helped an elderly woman across the street two days ago?

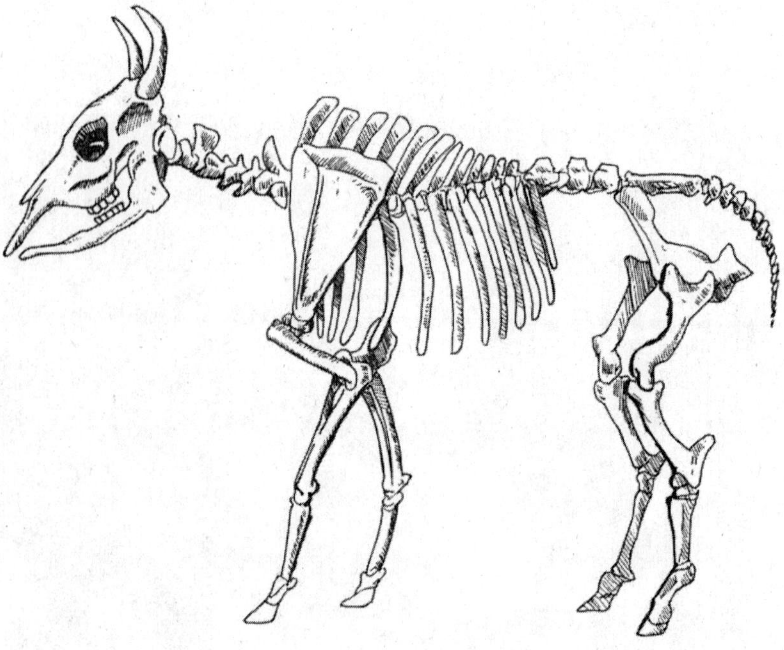

The Buddha tries, in the Digha Nikaya, to explain this difficulty with a simile. He shows that each new moment of time brings a different reality, but the birth of each new reality is dependent upon its predecessor. There is a sequence that forms a continuity between lives such that karma inexorably follows, yet properly speaking each successive reality is different from another.

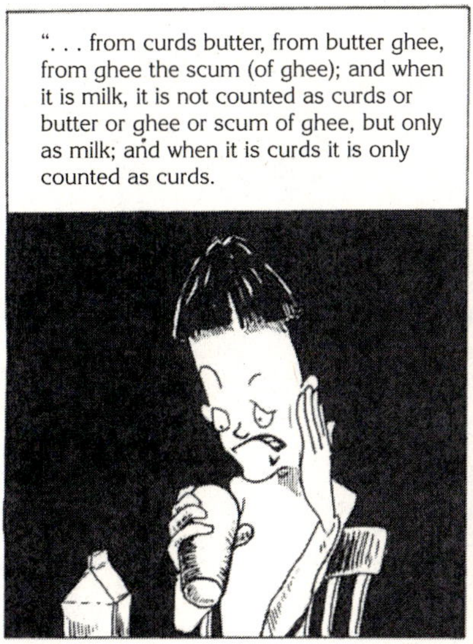

There is no self that unites these different "bundles of perception" (persons) through lifetimes, but each one is still causally connected to its previous reality. And this is how karma can work without appeal to the concept of atman. The milk necessarily precedes the existence of ghee; there is a causal connection between the two different substances. So too, past, present, and future lives are tied together by the sequential law of cause and effect.

A few hundred years after the Buddha's death, the Buddhist sage Nagasena attempted to clarify this puzzling doctrine for the argumentative Bactrian king Milinda. King Milinda seeks to understand how the doctrine of no-self can be reconciled with that of karma.
"When someone is reborn, Venerable Nagasena, is he the same as the one who just died, or is he another?"
"He is neither the same nor another."
"Give me a simile."
"If a man were to light a lamp, could it give light throughout the whole night?"
"Yes, it could."
"Is now the flame that burns in the first watch of the night the same as the one that burns in the second?"
"It is not the same."
"Or is the flame that burns in the second watch the same as the one that burns in the last one?"
"It is not the same."
"Do we then take it that there is one lamp in the first watch of the night, another in the second, and another again in the third?"
"No, it is because of just that one lamp that the light shines throughout the night."
"And so like the lamp, we must understand the juxtaposition of a series of successive lives. At rebirth one life arises, while another stops; but the two processes take place almost simultaneously (i.e., they are continuous). The ego does not continue, only the Khandas."

Another simile may also help us understand this difficult doctrine. Imagine a life span as a lit candle. Now take that candle and light another candle, immediately blowing out the first candle. Repeat this process several times, each time lighting a new candle and extinguishing the previous. It seems absurd to say that the flame at the end of the process is the same flame as the first lit candle. It is not one identical flame that gets passed along; in fact, the flame is different from itself at each moment even while it burns on one candle. But there is a definite causal relationship uniting the first and last candles. Karma links earlier and later lives together in the same way that the different flames are linked together, but there is no "one substance" (self) that continues throughout.

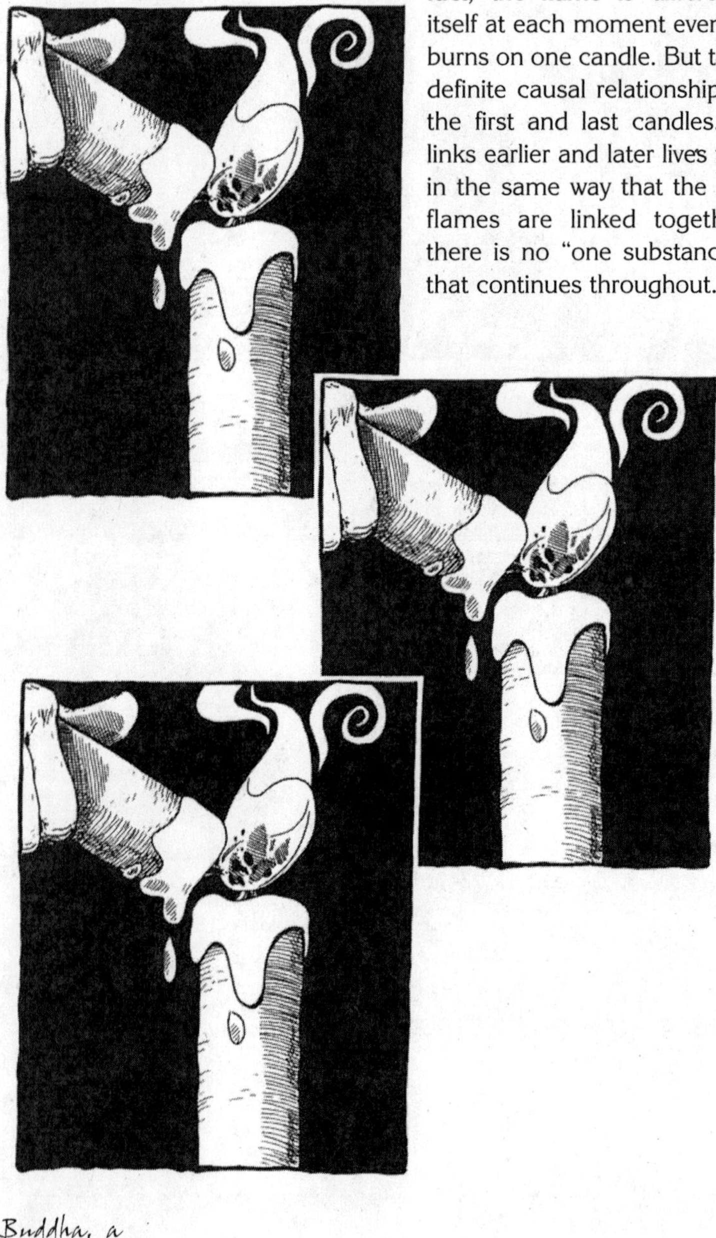

Having made these radical metaphysical changes to traditional Indian philosophy, the Buddha refused to engage in further metaphysical speculation and focused his energies on freeing people through moral action from the chains of suffering. Much of the Buddha's moral teachings presupposes this intricate metaphysics, but he knew that the masses of people who were uninitiated in the subtleties of Hindu scholarship could simply ignore these subtleties and move on to the process of healing themselves.

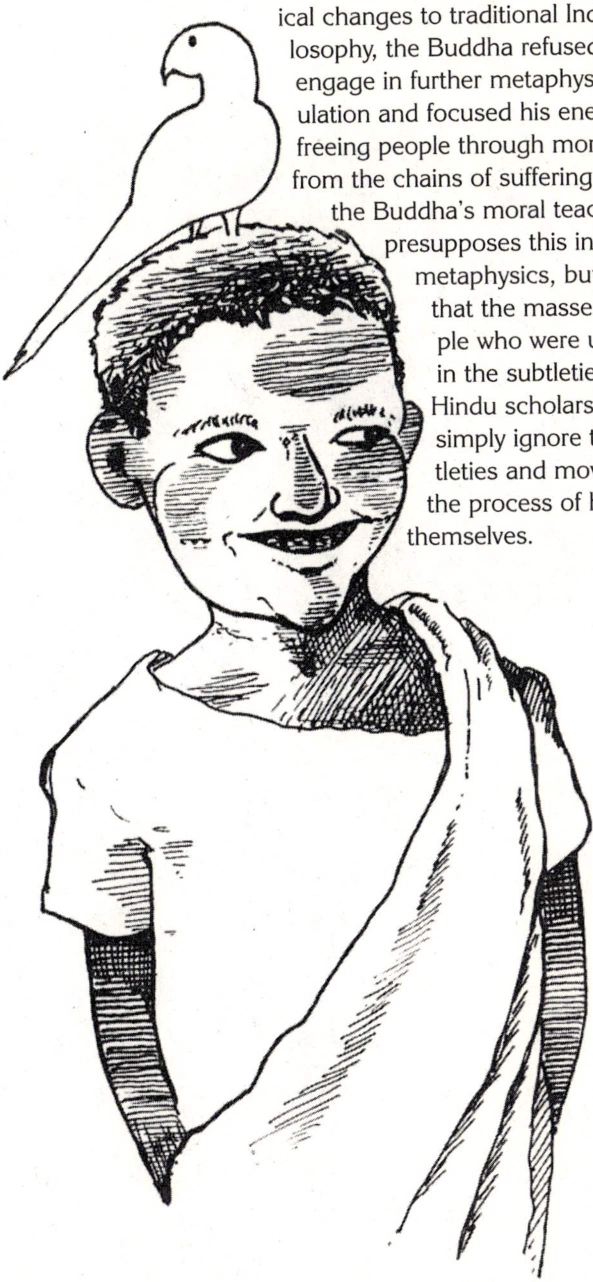

So, now that we have seen what the "wheel of becoming" actually is, let us find out how one escapes from it. For unlike most Western religions, the Buddha does not want immortality or everlasting life. On the contrary, Buddhism seeks to stop the afterlife. The goal of Buddhism is to be extinguished, to blow out one's flame.

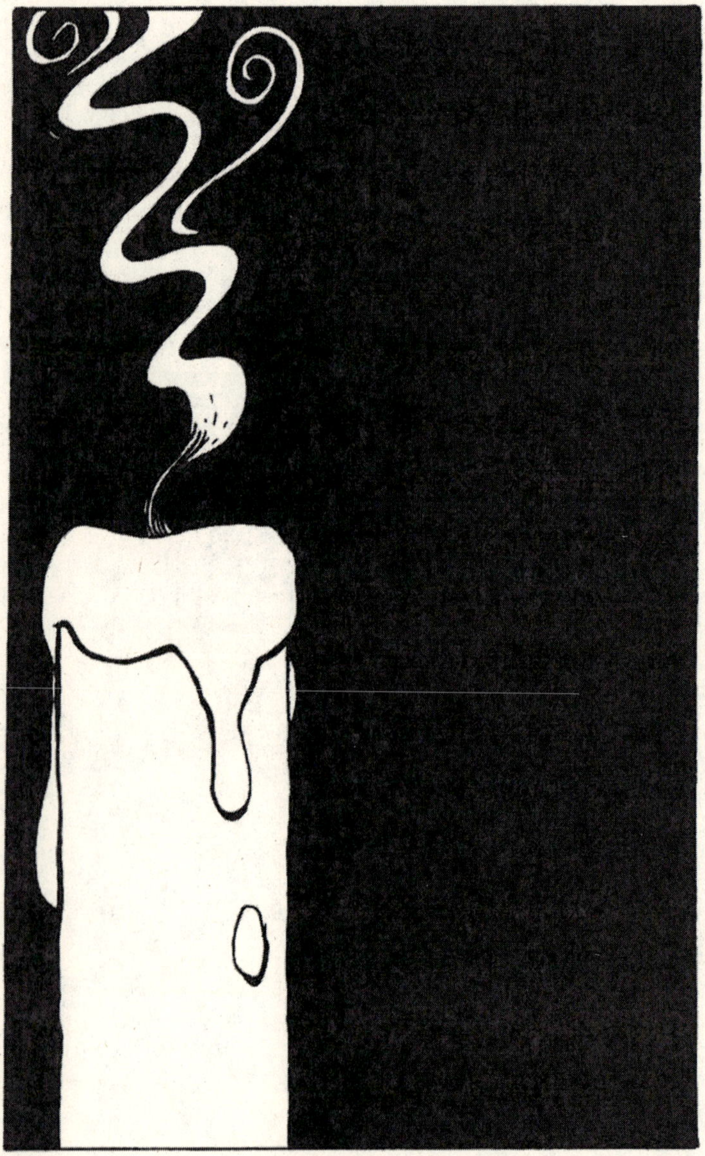

Chapter III

Nirvana and the Noble Truths

Though one must eventually develop deep philosophical powers of reflection, a doctorate in Hindu metaphysics is not a necessary prerequisite for enlightenment. The Buddha holds that one can embark upon the righteous path without first resolving every cosmic puzzle. Buddhism is a strenuously practical philosophy, which, similar to the attitude of Socrates in the West, stressed individual moral development over pure theory.

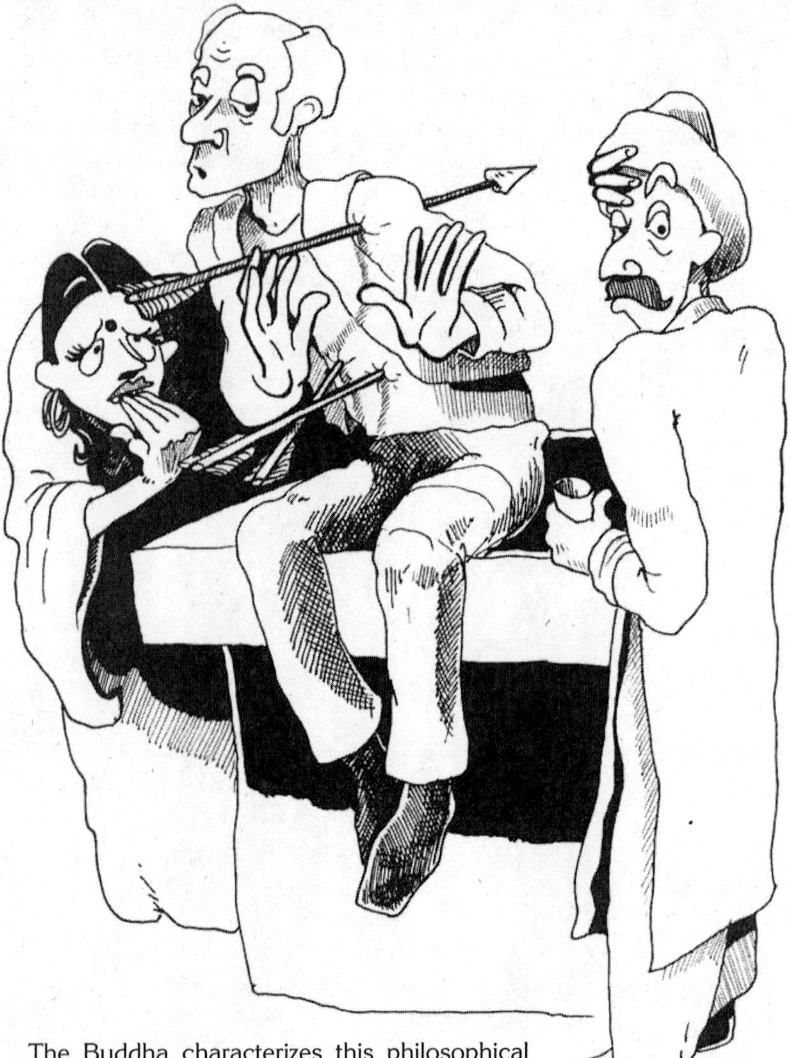

The Buddha characterizes this philosophical preference with an analogy in the Majjhima Nikaya text (chapter 63):

"Should anyone say that he does not wish to lead the righteous life under the Enlightened One, unless the Enlightened One first tells him whether the world is eternal or temporal, finite or infinite; whether the life principle is identical with the body, or sometimes different; whether the Perfect One continues after death, etc.—such a person would die, before the Perfect One could tell him all this. It is as if a man were pierced by a poisoned arrow, and his friends, companions, or near relations called in a surgeon, but that man should say, I will not have this arrow pulled out until I know who the man is that has wounded me: whether he is a noble, a prince, a citizen, or a servant; or whether he is tall, or short, or of medium height. Truly, such a man would die, before he could adequately learn all this."

In all of his thinking and teaching, the Buddha never loses sight of his pragmatic original mission, which is to find the cure for human suffering. The most important key to understanding the path to enlightenment is that set of Buddha's teachings (dharma) known as the Four Noble Truths.

Meditating beneath that tree in the Ganges Valley, Gautama awakened to the First Noble Truth, which is: All life is permeated with suffering (dukkha). To live is to suffer.

This appears at first to be a deeply pessimistic outlook, but the Buddha is simply stating that a variety of pains and misfortunes accompany the human condition. For example, in possessing a body every human being is open to the suffering of degeneration (getting sick, growing old, etc.), and having a family and friends means that we are all open to the pain of loss, disappointment, and even betrayal.

In the Anguttara Nikaya text, Buddha vividly sketches the unsatisfactory (dukkha) quality of life:

"Did you ever see in the world a man or woman, eighty, ninety, or a hundred years old, frail, crooked as a gable-roof, bent down, supported on a staff, with tottering steps, infirm, youth long since fled, with broken teeth, grey and scanty hair, or bald-headed, wrinkled, with blotched limbs? And did the thought never come to you, that you also are subject to decay, that you cannot escape it?"

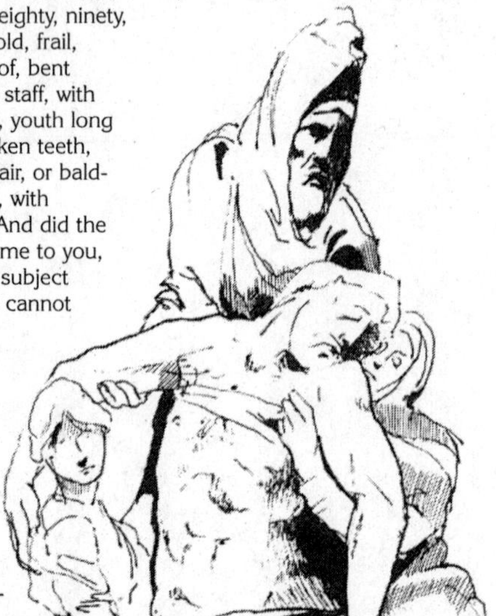

"Did you never see in the world a man or woman, who being sick, afflicted, and grievously ill, and wallowing in one's own filth, was lifted up by some people and put to bed by others? And did the thought never come to you, that you also are subject to disease, that you cannot escape it?

"Did you never see in the world the corpse of a man or a woman, one or two or three days after death, swollen up, blue-black in color, and full of corruption? And did the thought never come to you, that you also are subject to death, that you cannot escape it?" (Book 3, chapter 35)

This morose perspective is not merely the product of a melancholy disposition, for the Buddha has a sophisticated psychological and biological rationale for the pain that accompanies all human existence. The avenues by which these painful experiences travel are the five aggregates that we have already encountered: body, feeling, perception, disposition, and consciousness.

These five aggregates are the physiological and psychological faculties through which we both passively receive the world and actively partake in that world; the "person" or "self" is more identifiable with the aggregates or "bundles of experience" than with a traditional "ghost in the machine" type of soul. These aggregates of experience are the "organs" of pleasure and pain, and it is in relation to pleasure and pain that human craving can begin to arise. The Buddha summarizes the First Noble Truth in the Digha-Nikaya text:

> "Birth is suffering; Decay is suffering; Death is suffering; Sorrow, Lamentation, Pain, Grief, and Despair are suffering; not to get what one desires is suffering; in short: the Five Aggregates of Existence are Suffering" (chapter 22).

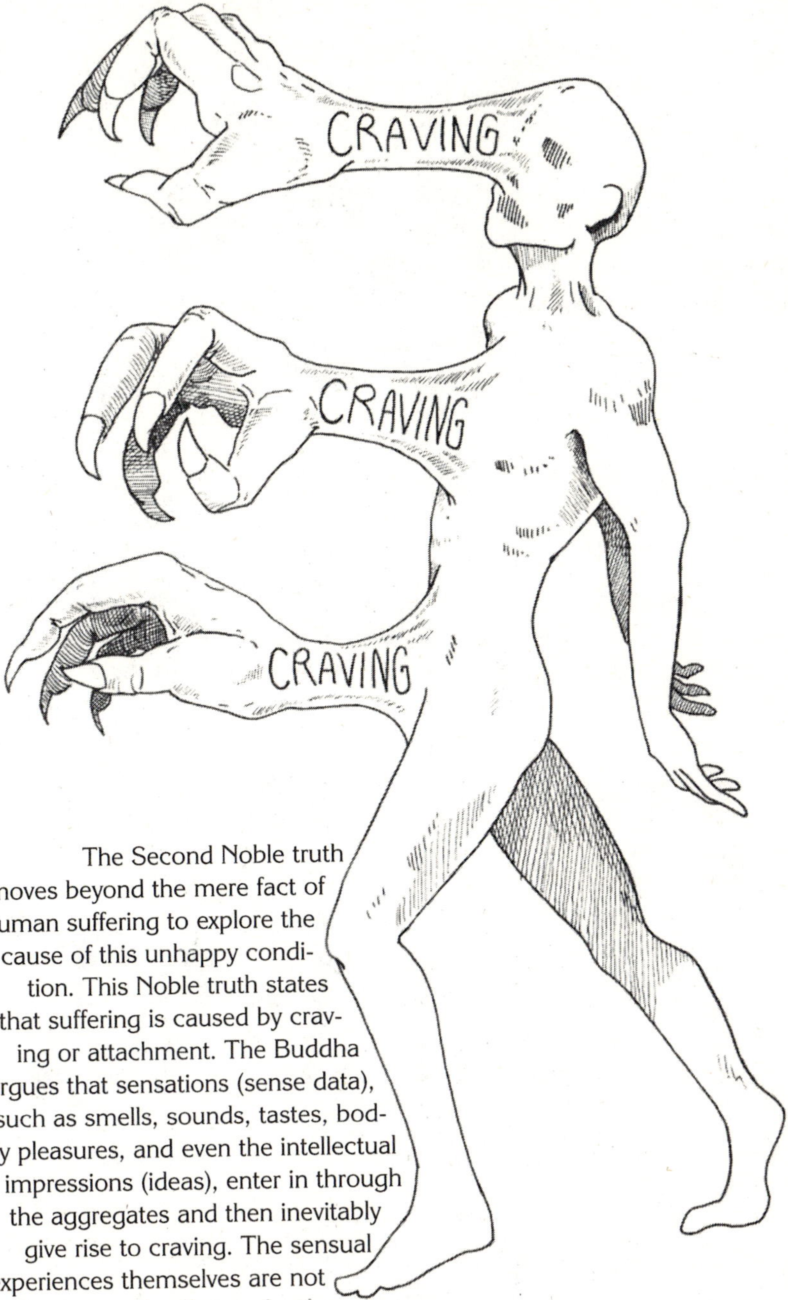

The Second Noble truth moves beyond the mere fact of human suffering to explore the cause of this unhappy condition. This Noble truth states that suffering is caused by craving or attachment. The Buddha argues that sensations (sense data), such as smells, sounds, tastes, bodily pleasures, and even the intellectual impressions (ideas), enter in through the aggregates and then inevitably give rise to craving. The sensual experiences themselves are not the cause of suffering, for they are inherently neutral phenomena. It is, rather, the fixation or clinging response that we take up regarding these sense impressions.

For example, it is not the sensual experiences that money affords us—fine food, fancy clothes, travel, new cars, and so on—nor is it the material objects themselves that are inherently pernicious. It is the craving, wanting, desiring appetites, which become obsessed with repeating and sustaining those experiences, that actually cause the suffering, in this case, of greed. Suffering flows from clinging attachment, which mistakes impermanent things and sensations for lasting and permanent realities. Attachment is a confusion, in the mind and the heart, that tries to capture or solidify that which is forever in flux.

In the Majjhima Nikaya, Buddha develops the Second Noble Truth:

"If namely, when perceiving a visible form, a sound, odor, taste, bodily contact, or idea in the mind, the object is pleasant, one is attracted, and if unpleasant, one is repelled. Thus, whatever kind of feeling one experiences—pleasant, unpleasant, or indifferent—one approves of and cherishes the feeling and clings to it; and while doing so, lust springs up; but lust for feelings means clinging to existence; and on clinging to existence depends the process of becoming; on the process of becoming depends future birth; and dependent on birth are decay and death, sorrow, lamentation, pain, grief, and despair. Thus arises this whole mass of suffering" (chapter 38).

The sensations that are always flowing in upon us become problematic only when we seek to hold on to the pleasant experiences, when we try to capture the ephemeral. Conversely, when we feel indignant and personally injured or offended by the unpleasant sensations, we have mistakenly reified our self into an object (soul), when we are really nothing but a process of changing aggregates. That is to say, we have made the mistake that Buddha believes the traditional Hindus have made; namely, we have forgotten that we too (our selves) are impermanent transitory realities. As an impermanent transitory reality, I can only be injured or indignant if I cling to myself, if I think of myself as a substance enduring through time. Craving, for the Buddha, is both an emotional passion and an intellectual misconception about reality. The suffering is caused when we falsely attribute "absolute" reality where there is only "relative" reality.

The Third Noble Truth states that the cure for suffering is nonattachment, or the cessation of craving. Freedom is not the renunciation of all emotions and feelings; it is the ability to rise above the incoming sensations. One still feels pain and pleasure, but one no longer clings to these fluctuating experiences. In the Dhammapada text, Buddha explains:

"The enlightened ones, at all times, surrender in truth all attachments. The holy spend not idle words on things of desire. When pleasure or pain comes to them, the wise feel above pleasure and pain" (chapter 6).

When the sensual perceptions and the mental ideas flow through the five aggregates that we conventionally call "Buddha," they continue flowing in their natural course without a clinging ego chasing after them. This detachment leaves no fertile soil for craving to take root. In the Samyutta Nikaya text, Buddha explains that detachment stems from the philosophical realization of impermanence:

"Be it in the past, present, or future: whosoever of the monks or priests regards the delightful and pleasurable things of this world as impermanent, miserable, and without an Ego (anatman), as a disease and sorrow, it is he who overcomes the craving" (chapter 12).

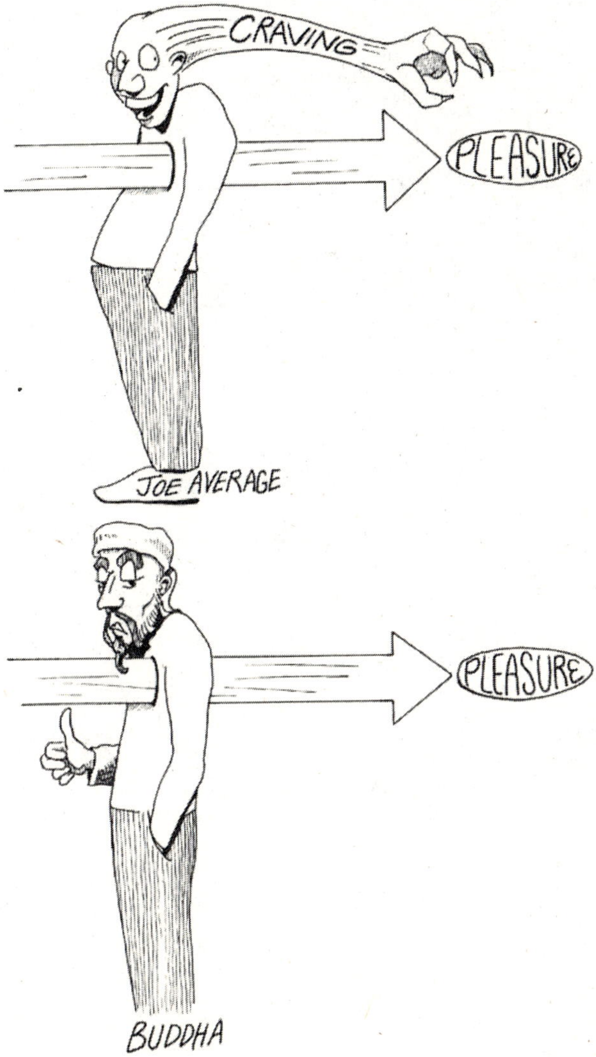

"He who knows that this body is the foam of a wave, the shadow of a mirage, he breaks the sharp arrows of Mara (the personification of temptation), concealed in the flowers of sensuous passions and, unseen by Yama (the personification of painful death), he goes on and follows his path" (Dhammapada, chapter 4).

This leads to the Fourth Noble Truth, which is really more like eight more truths masquerading as one. The cure for suffering, characterized in the Third Noble Truth as nonattachment, has eight steps or stages of practical realization, referred to as the Noble Eightfold Path. The Eightfold Path is a set of prescriptive attitudes and activities that will lead to the extinction of suffering; it is the path of freedom.

In the Samyutta Nikaya, the Buddha sets forth the facets of the righteous path:

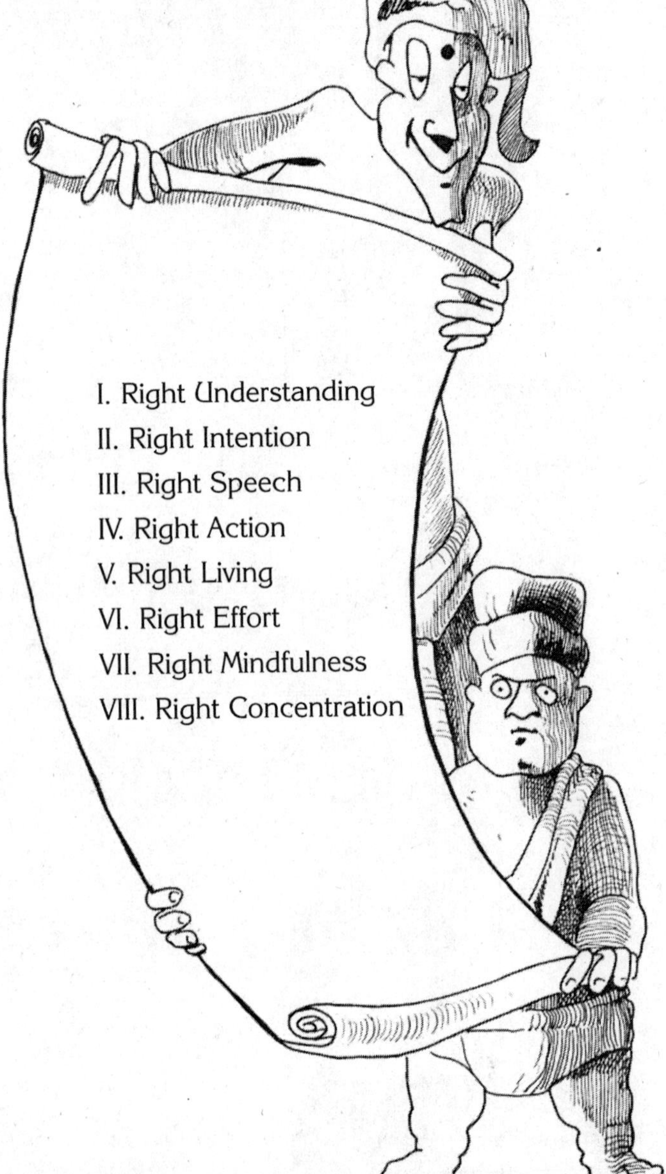

These eight maxims steer the searcher between the two pitfalls of extreme indulgence on the one hand and extreme asceticism on the other. The eight injunctions form the ethical details of that more general life principle, the Middle Way. It is worth exploring a few of the eight modes in greater depth.

Right Understanding: Similar to Socrates' famous position that the good life is the "examined" life, the Buddha believes that intellectual and emotional confusion must be grappled with on a daily basis. Right Understanding occurs when one pierces through the veil of naive consciousness (thinking of ourselves as Ego) to arrive at the true nature of things. The Buddha, and Socrates after him, understood that clarity of thought was most difficult regarding issues in which the passions had a strong interest. One has to be especially vigilant when it comes to the temptations that can arise from the aggregate sensations.

Thus, in the Majjhima Nikaya and elsewhere, one finds fairly predictable lists of merit and demerit. Part of Right Understanding is sorting out demerits (destruction of living beings, stealing, lying, frivolous talk, etc.) from merits (abstaining from killing, abstaining from stealing, abstaining from lying, etc.).

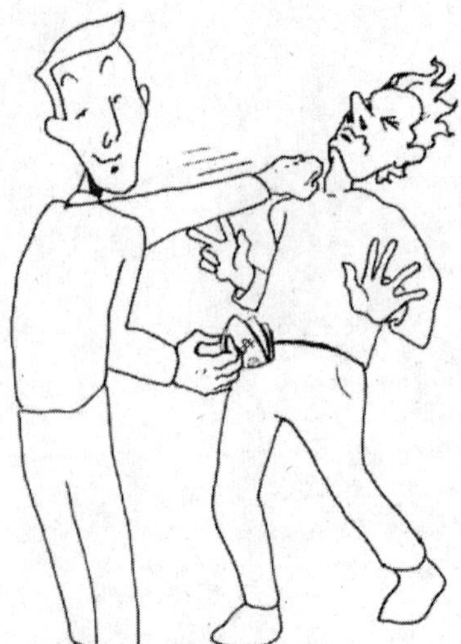

What is more interesting than these piety lists, however, is that original Buddhism treats intellectual rigor as a virtue and ignorance as a sin. Some later sects of Buddhism have shared similar hostilities with Western religions towards the intellect, claiming that ignorant faith is more important than logical thought. Right Understanding is the thoughtful discernment that helps a person see past the quick-fix gratifications to long-range karmic implications. Critical thinking, for the Buddha, is part of the moral path to freedom, for it allows one to recognize internal confusion.

Right Living: Many Western interpretations of Buddhism characterize the devotee as severely ascetic—refusing all pleasures and comforts—and ultimately becoming a kind of unfeeling self-negating zombie. Whereas some followers feel the need for such draconian measures, the Buddha himself never claimed that the path to enlightenment was self-torture.

This makes perfect sense when we understand that pleasure and pain are inherently neutral, and immoral living arises only from the ego attachments that tend to follow them. Therefore, one can enjoy—with moderation—all the earthly pleasures that any human has available. Poverty is not a necessary requirement for enlightenment; it is but another harmful extreme like opulence.

For the Buddha, Right Living can contain prosperity if it is gained honestly without fraud or deception. Legitimately acquired wealth can be a source of happiness as long as greed (craving and ego-consciousness) does not throw one back into the quagmire of suffering. Economic prosperity can give one the happiness that accompanies freedom from debt. But that prosperity cannot have injured another, for then it will not be able to give one freedom from blame.

Right Mindfulness: Mental discipline is crucial for achieving freedom. The early training that Gautama received in yoga meditation, plus his own "mindfulness," continued to play an important role in his mature philosophy. The Buddha, after all, had used these meditation practices that fateful day beneath the Bodhi tree. Meditation is a deep form of psychological and physiological retraining, which allows one to perceive and reflect upon the facets of reality that are frequently masked and confused in the normal conscious state.

Intense concentration and profound tranquility blend together for the master yogi, and in this state she is reminded (through "experience" rather than discursive description) what freedom from worldly suffering is actually like.

Meditation is a method of inquiry that comprises four subjects of contemplation; these are the four fundamentals of mindfulness set forth in the Digha Nikaya.

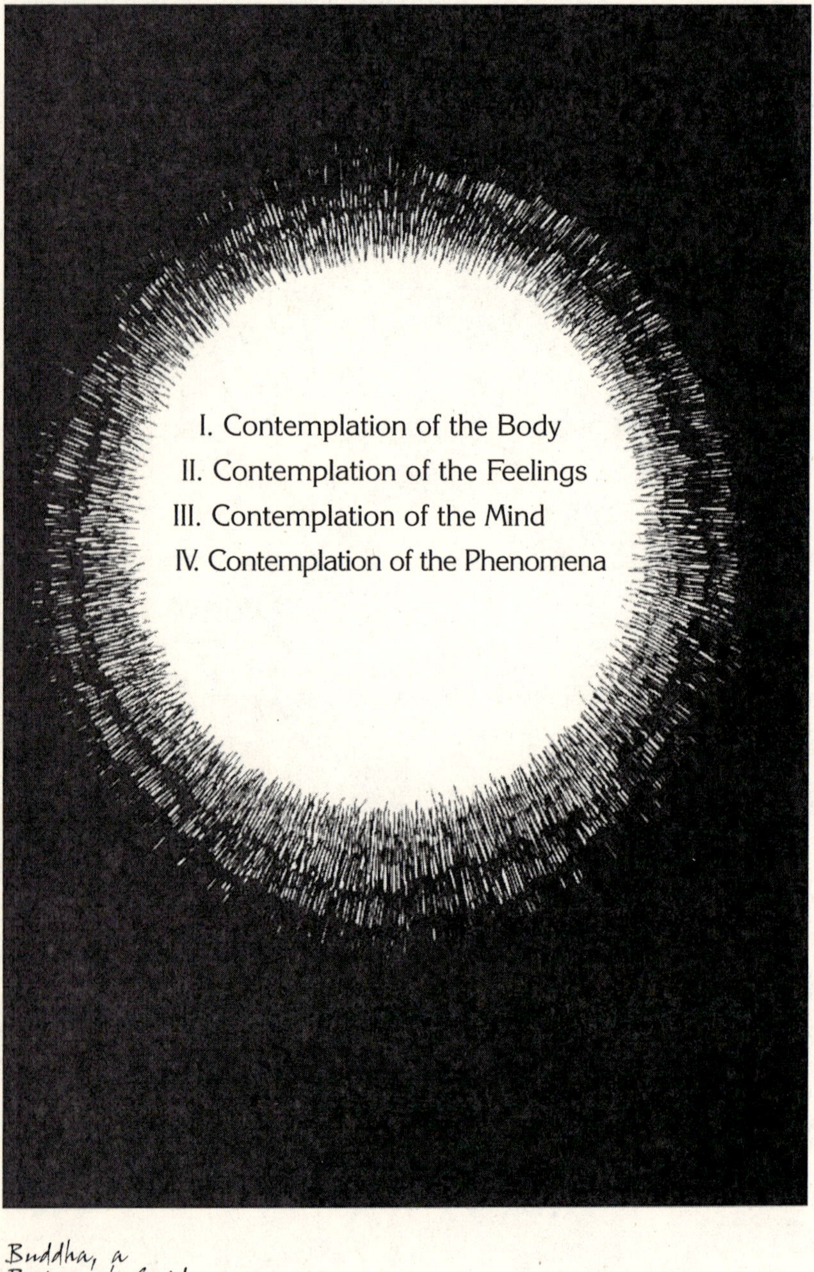

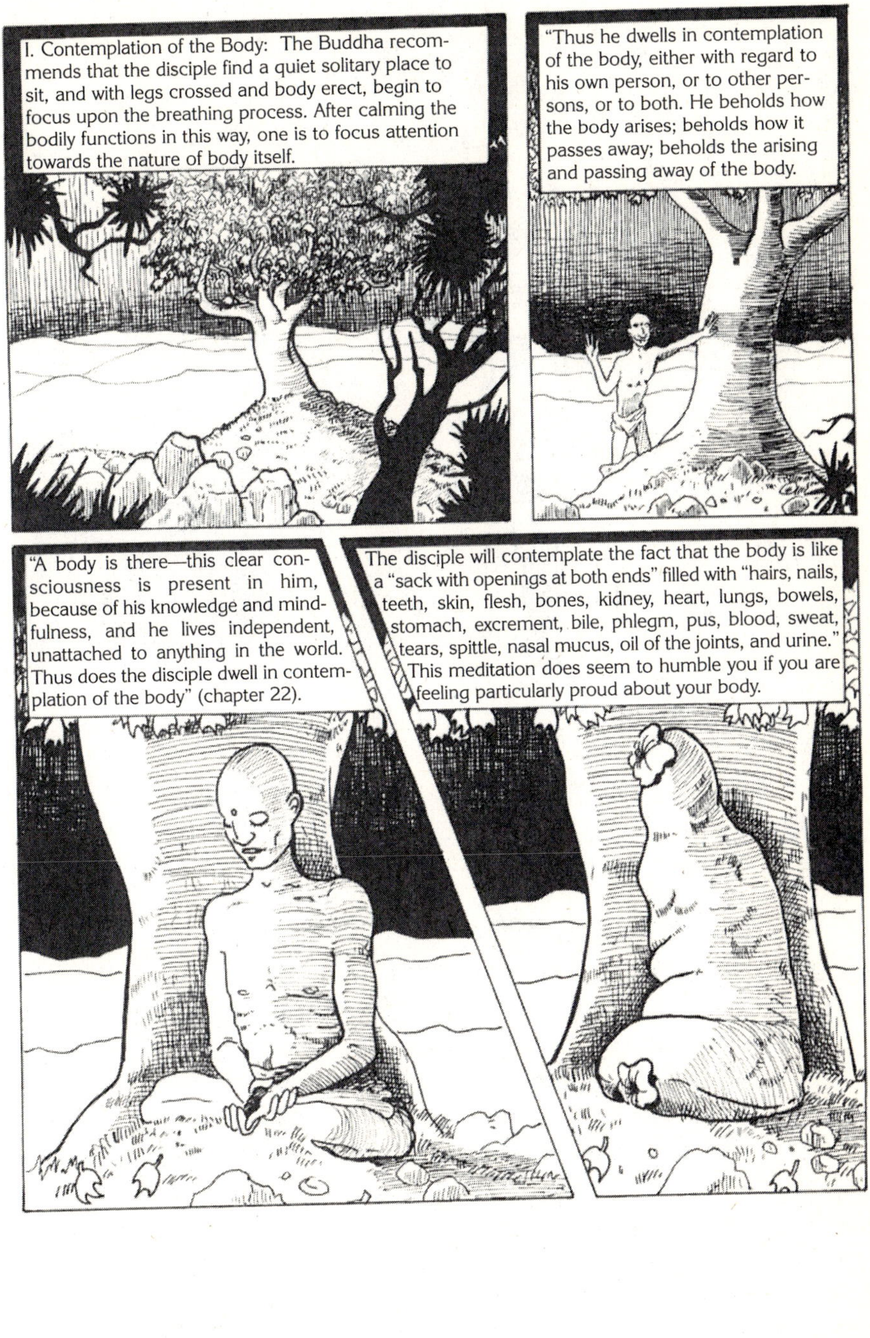
I. Contemplation of the Body: The Buddha recommends that the disciple find a quiet solitary place to sit, and with legs crossed and body erect, begin to focus upon the breathing process. After calming the bodily functions in this way, one is to focus attention towards the nature of body itself.
"Thus he dwells in contemplation of the body, either with regard to his own person, or to other persons, or to both. He beholds how the body arises; beholds how it passes away; beholds the arising and passing away of the body.
"A body is there—this clear consciousness is present in him, because of his knowledge and mindfulness, and he lives independent, unattached to anything in the world. Thus does the disciple dwell in contemplation of the body" (chapter 22).
The disciple will contemplate the fact that the body is like a "sack with openings at both ends" filled with "hairs, nails, teeth, skin, flesh, bones, kidney, heart, lungs, bowels, stomach, excrement, bile, phlegm, pus, blood, sweat, tears, spittle, nasal mucus, oil of the joints, and urine." This meditation does seem to humble you if you are feeling particularly proud about your body.

With similarly penetrating honesty, the disciple continues with the fundamentals of mindfulness: II. Contemplation of the Feelings; III. Contemplation of the Mind; and IV. Contemplation of the Phenomena.

The Buddha summarizes the concept of Right Mindfulness in the Majjhima Nikaya (chapter 125):

"Just as the elephant hunter drives a huge stake into the ground and chains the wild elephant to it by the neck, in order to drive out from him his wonted forest ways and wishes, his forest unruliness, obstinacy, and violence, and to accustom him to the environment of the village, and to teach him such good behavior as is required amongst men:—in like manner also has the noble disciple to fix his mind firmly to these four fundamentals of mindfulness, so that he may drive out of himself his wonted worldly ways and wishes, his wonted worldly unruliness, obstinacy and violence, and win to the True and realize Nirvana."

We have now examined, with some detail, three out of the eight steps of the Fourth Noble Truth. An important general point should now be raised regarding the overall character of Buddhist ethics.

The implementation of the Eightfold Path should not be carried out in a dogmatic, legalistic fashion. The pathway is not an inflexible moral law dispensed by some otherworldly Judge, nor is it an unbending absolute duty dispensed from pure reason. As in the other areas of the Buddha's philosophy, here too the follower must attempt to avoid the lure of permanent absolutes.

Just as one is to refrain from viewing oneself as eternal, so too one is to refrain from thinking of ethical codes as eternal. This does not lead the Buddha into the swamps of ethical relativism (yet another "extreme"). In other words, once the Buddha claims that ethical decisions are dependent upon the "context" within which they arise, he is not thereby thrown into an "anything goes" morality. This is because the rightness or wrongness of any activity will be measured in terms of whether it respectively contributes to freedom (nirvana) or slavery (the wheel of becoming). And the same activity committed in two different contexts or by two different people can have two different implications for freedom. In this way, the Buddha's ethical philosophy has a liquid quality, an adaptability to situations. Ethics is the gateway to freedom, but if taken too dogmatically, it can itself become a roadblock.

A classic example to illustrate the importance of context in moral activity is the following scenario. Imagine that you are living in Nazi-occupied Europe and you are harboring a Jewish family in your basement.
Several SS officers making routine inquiries come to your door asking if you have seen any Jews in the vicinity.
Now, if the moral rule "Thou shalt not lie" is lived as an absolute—that is, as an inflexible law—you might be compelled to reveal the hidden family. But of course the deeper ethic should lead you to lie through your teeth.
JEWS EH? GOSH... NEVER HEARD OF 'EM. SORRY.
Compassion, not legalistic duty, leads one to the right activity. This illustrates how a slavish dedication to doctrinaire morality has the potential to thwart true morality. And it is for these reasons that Buddha wants a Middle Way of context morality rather than the extremes of absolutism and relativism.

"Be moral and virtuous without being made of morals or virtues" (Majjhima Nikaya, chapter 2). Compassion flows from the realization of human suffering and the impermanence of all things. Even our "enemies," for example, begin to arouse our compassion when we realize that they too are trapped by suffering. With this notion Buddha sought to rescue morality from the empty formalities of the Brahmins. Without a cultivated heart of compassion, rules and rituals are blind.

Next we must examine the goal of the moral life: nirvana. Nirvana is one of those commonly invoked and commonly misunderstood concepts. The Buddha speaks of nirvana in two different senses: nirvana with the substrate (saupadisesa), and nirvana without the substrate (anupadisesa). We must sort out these two different forms of freedom.

Literally, nirvana means "going out" or "extinguishing" a flame, and we frequently find the Buddha playing with this image in his sermons. But what exactly is "going out" and what is this talk of a "substrate"?

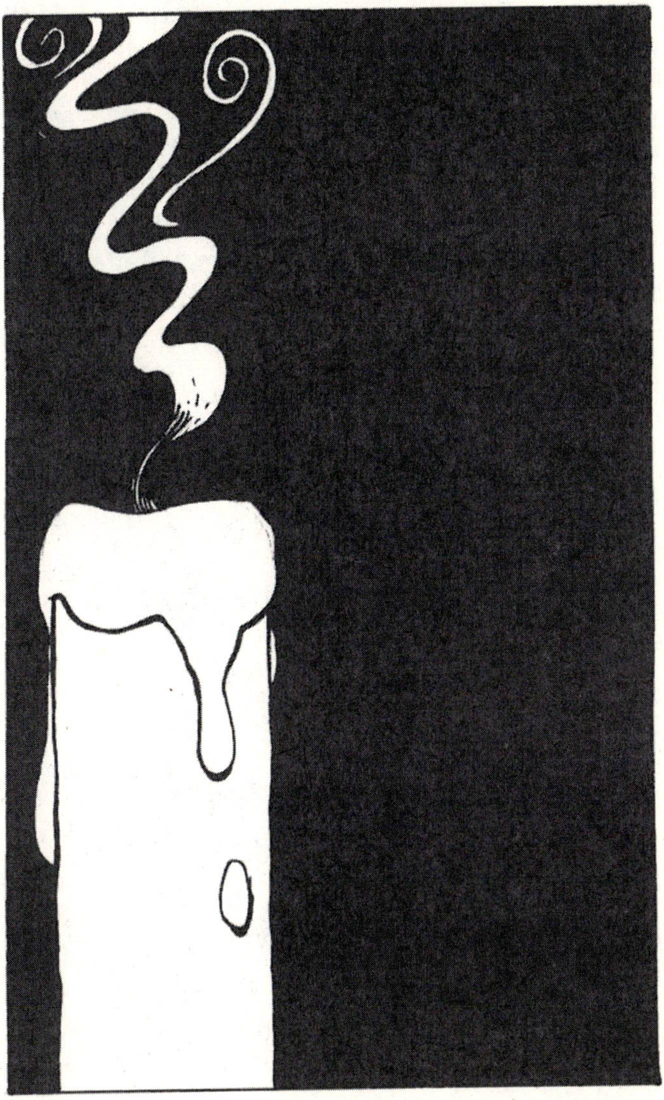

In the Itivuttaka, Buddha explains the concept of freedom with the substrate left. He describes the disciple who has effectively detached from his craving impulses, and he states that this individual has actually achieved freedom in this lifetime:

"He retains his five senses, through which, as they are not yet destroyed, he experiences pleasant and unpleasant sensations and feels pleasure and pain. This cessation of craving, hate, and confusion is called the nirvana with the substrate left" (Book 2, chapter 44).

Nirvana with substrate is living and experiencing through the five senses like everyone else, but no craving or confusion stems from those sense perceptions. "Substrate" refers to the underlying five aggregates that constitute each living person. Some interpreters have been confused about this form of nirvana, claiming that the Buddha is referring to the tranquil state of meditative trance that the trained yogi obtains. But on close examination, one finds this form of freedom characterized as an active life, one engaged in daily affairs.

The Buddha himself is an example of nirvana with the substrate left, because during his life he still functioned like any organism (via the five aggregates) yet he remained above the manipulations that frequently accompany these experiences.

"For he whose mind is well trained in the ways that lead to light, who surrenders the bondage of attachments and finds joy in his freedom from bondage, who free from the darkness of passions shines pure in radiance of light, even in this mortal life he enjoys the immortal nirvana" (Dhammapada, chapter 6).

In the Anguttara Nikaya (Book 3, chapter 53), Buddha again describes the individual, who has realized the ephemeral character of reality and recognized the traps of desire, as achieving freedom in this lifetime:

"Thus is nirvana immediate, visible in this life, inviting, attractive, and comprehensible to the wise."

The usual course of events is that an impression, say self-satisfaction, enters into the individual and then ego-consciousness quickly leaps in to coddle and indulge the impression, thereby transforming it into "pride." One who lives nirvana is able to receive the impressions (the "substrate" of experience) but stop the second step—the entrance of the ego-consciousness. This violation of the usual course of events is possible because the person finally understands the causal mechanisms at work on and through her—she understands her own psychology. And through incredible discipline, she has practiced a lifetime of this detachment process. The Buddha actually describes this rare individual as the person "who goes upstream" rather than succumbing to the normal flow of attachment.

So, this form of nirvana is a kind of "transcendence" but it is not, contrary to some interpretations, transcendence to an otherworldly heaven. One psychologically rises above the muck and mire of mundane existence, but there is no ascension to a supernatural realm. This consideration leads us to the even more controversial form, nirvana without substrate.

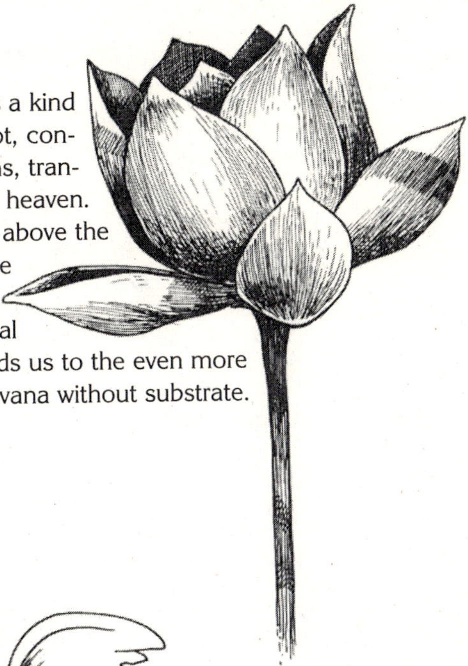

In addition to the freedom attainable in this lifetime, the Buddha talks of an ultimate goal, often connected to the death of the enlightened person. This connection has led many, both later Buddhists and Western interpreters, to equate "nirvana without substrate" with an afterlife in a heavenly realm.

In the Dhammapada, Buddha describes this more complete form of freedom:

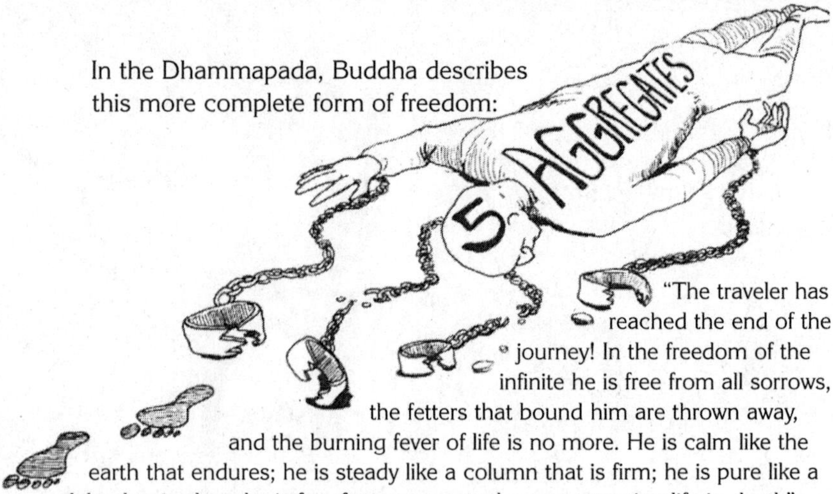

"The traveler has reached the end of the journey! In the freedom of the infinite he is free from all sorrows, the fetters that bound him are thrown away, and the burning fever of life is no more. He is calm like the earth that endures; he is steady like a column that is firm; he is pure like a lake that is clear; he is free from samsara, the ever returning life-in-death" (chapter 7).

One needs to be careful here about assuming a doctrine of heavenly immortality. Freedom with substrate means nonattachment with sense impressions still passing through the body and consciousness, whereas freedom without substrate means that even these sense impressions have finally ceased. Thus nirvana in this case is not simply the "going out" or "extinguishing" of craving, it is the "going out" of all felt experiences. And it is here that the yogic trance does in fact give one the momentary cessation of all sense experience. That is to say, for brief periods the yogi can know what it is like to be dead—to be without substrate (the aggregates).

There is nothing, however, in this doctrine about surviving after death. Nonetheless, many of Buddha's disciples felt compelled at this precise juncture to ask about the afterlife; the issue seems to cry out for some speculation.
A student of the Buddha, Vacchagotta, asked the Master (Majjhima Nikaya, chapter 72):
"Where does the enlightened person go after death?"
"It is impossible to say whether he is altogether annihilated or whether he is reborn again."
"But surely he continues on in some form?"
"Does a flame 'go somewhere' or 'continue' after is has burned all of its fuel?"
"No."
"Just as the fire is extinguished after all fuel is consumed, so too the enlightened one is extinguished after the aggregates (body, feeling, perception, disposition, and consciousness) are no more."

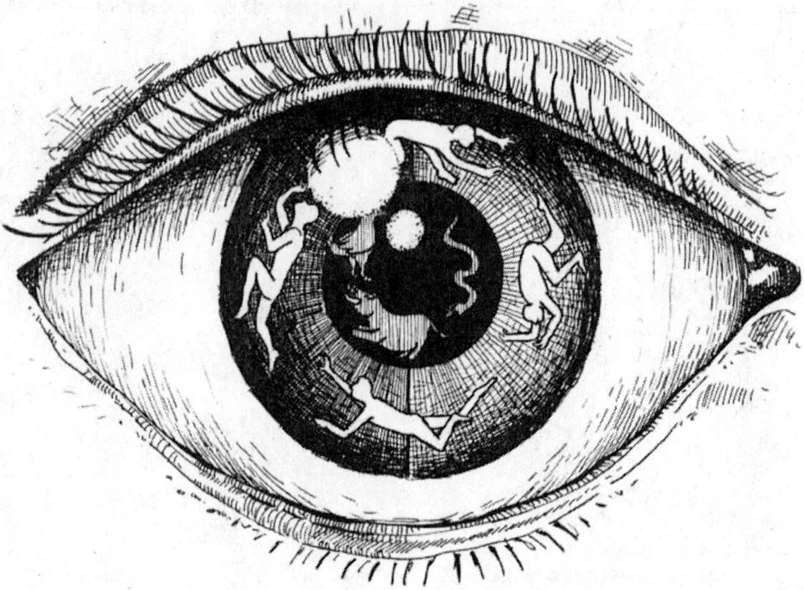

Ultimately, the Buddha is suggesting that it is absurd and meaningless to ask: "Where does a flame go when it goes out?" And it is likewise absurd to engage in metaphysical speculation about events after death. Since we cannot have a full experience of ourselves after death, we cannot claim any real knowledge about this condition. The Buddha teaches that we must remain neutral on such questions and again walk the "middle way" between the dogma of afterlife belief and the dogma of annihilation. Indeed, so strong was Buddha's agnosticism about such metaphysical issues that he even refused to say whether nirvana or freedom itself would last forever. Just as the sensual world and self are truly ephemeral, so too even freedom may be only transitory.

Nirvana and the Noble Truths

Chapter IV

The Evolution of Buddhism

The Buddha died around 480 BCE having already won many devotees with his compelling discourses. For approximately fifty years after his enlightenment, he traveled the Ganges Valley teaching people that freedom from suffering was within their grasp. As he was dying, his closest friend, Ananda, expressed worries about how the community could continue the philosophy after the passing of the great Teacher. The Buddha responded by claiming that he had already taught them everything he knew; he had not held back any secrets. Therefore, he explained, the devotees would do fine without him. He said, "Ananda, be a lamp unto yourself, be a refuge unto yourself; seek not any outside help in this matter." His last words, like all his teachings, are inspired by his overriding respect for human potential.

The historical Buddha affected several important philosophical revolutions during his lifetime. He challenged the ritualistic religions around him, arguing that morality and happiness are not the result of animal sacrifices and hollow ceremonial gestures. Ritual observance is only valid when it is an outward sign of an inner compassion.

He deplored the caste system and attempted to negate its pernicious bondage by arguing that the path to freedom is open to all who wish to pursue it. Nirvana recognizes no hierarchy but diligence.

The Buddha developed "the middle way" and thereby explained that neither asceticism (self-denial) nor hedonism (self-indulgence) is inherently righteous, because detachment is more achievable through moderation. Both self-indulgence and self-denial are too bound up with the "self" to be successful.

Finally, he tempered the metaphysical flights of those who squander their thoughts on the unknowable and those who invent spirits and egos where none exist. He refused to engage in scholarly debates about the afterlife and other such issues on the grounds that such issues are not open to experience and they can distract one from the business of working out one's own enlightenment.

Shortly after the Buddha's death, the adherents began to fracture into diverse groups, each sect emphasizing a different nuance of the Teacher's message and life.

A series of councils met in the centuries after the Teacher's death to iron out doctrinal issues, the most famous of which seems to have been organized around 250 BCE by the converted emperor Asoka (circa 272–236).

According to legend, Asoka sent missionaries out of the Indian subcontinent, most notably south to Sri Lanka (Ceylon), and began the eventual spread of Buddhism throughout Asia. In Sri Lanka, the teachings of the Buddha were compiled into the Pali Canon (a corpus about ten times the length of the Bible), and it is these scriptures, divided into five groups or Nikayas, that seem to present us with the most accurate version of Gautama's teachings (together with the Chinese Agamas). Innumerably more texts, in various languages, have found their way into the Buddhist corpus over the centuries, and Buddhism has been radically transformed by every culture that embraces it. But the group that held fast to these earliest scriptures is usually referred to as Hinayana (the smaller path), and the most notable subsect (perhaps because it has endured in Southeast Asia) is known as the Theravada school (doctrine of the elders).

The discourses of the historical Buddha are collectively characterized as "dharma," but, as with most other great teachers, a set of subsequent texts began to arise after Gautama's death. These later texts are analyses of, and reflections on, the original dharma; they seem to be "secondary works" that found their way into the Buddhist canon. These philosophical treatises are known as "abhidharma" (special dharma), and they quickly gave rise to deep divisions in the ranks of the faithful.

Besides Theravada, other early Hinayana schools include the Sarvastivada and the Sautrantika. Not only did these sects disagree about whether the dharma or abhidharma were primary or secondary sources of wisdom, they also began to divide strongly on metaphysical issues.

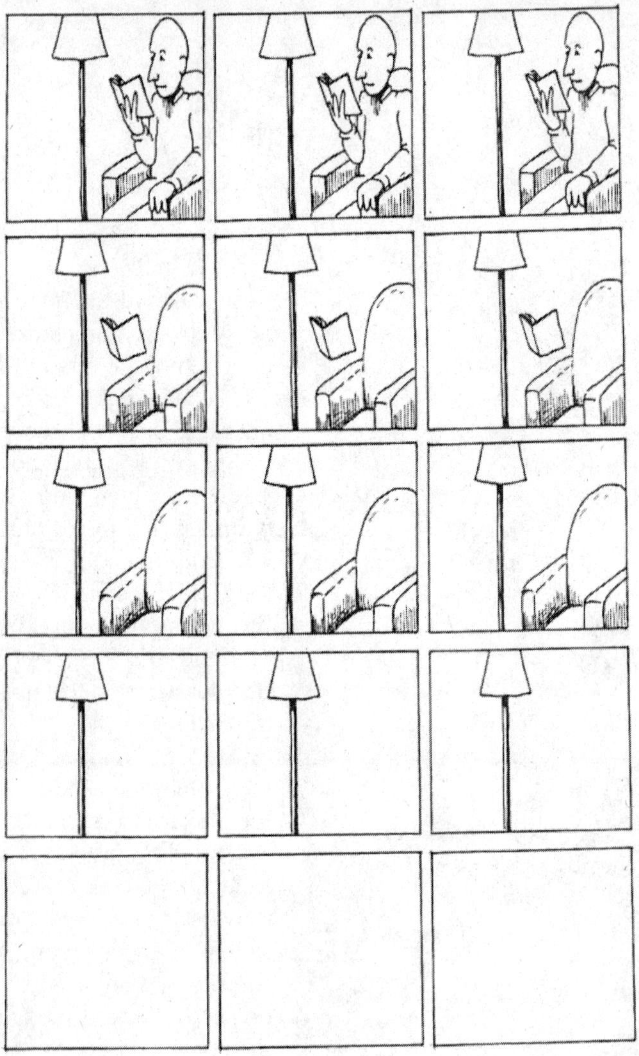

Trying to understand the Buddha's difficult doctrine of "no-self," the Sautrantikas argued that all moments follow each other with no underlying connection; each moment is completely unconnected to the previous moment and the future moment. The moments that you, the reader, spend reading this book seem to be tied together by the underlying identity of yourself—you seem to persist through the changes. But the Sautrantikas, following Buddha's rejection of the self, claimed that there was no underlying identity from one moment to the next. Therefore, they concluded, there is no cause and effect relationship through time.

In a game of billiards, for example, one billiard ball seems to be caused to move by another earlier moving billiard ball, but in reality we have two completely isolated moments that happen to be joined together in time but share no causal communication with each other. But the denial of causality is dangerously close to a denial of karma, and as such this development in Buddhist philosophy may be seen as a suspicious departure from Gautama's original teachings.

The Sarvastivadins likewise struggled with these same issues and tried to explain how causality could still link moments together in a way that accounts for the regularity of nature that we readily observe. As we have seen, central to Buddhism is the idea of the impermanence of all things. Yet the world is not a chaos of unrelated moments haphazardly thrown together. Babies grow into adults, seasons follow one another predictably, and politicians become corrupt.

Sarvastivadins attempted to explain this phenomenon of continuity in the midst of impermanence by arguing that some "essence" or "substance" (svabhava) must persist through the alterations. In doing so, they fell back into the metaphysical trap of postulating semipermanent entities that supposedly endure behind the curtain of impermanence. This metaphysical mistake is precisely the sort of error that led Hindus to postulate a spiritual ego (atman) behind their impermanent lives, and we have already seen that Gautama had little tolerance for this position.

Ultimately, the scholastic Buddhists of this ilk unwittingly sold out Gautama's emphasis on practical philosophy. Strains of later Buddhism, however, have managed to avoid the pitfalls of bad metaphysics while remaining true to the practical wisdom of the early discourses.

Contrasted with Hinayana (now Theravada) Buddhism is the more popular and heterogeneous school named Mahayana (the larger path). This larger (and younger) path bases much of its Buddhism on a loose confederation of texts known as the "Perfection of Wisdom" sutras (Prajnaparamita sutras). Most of the Buddhism known to us in the West is Mahayana—Tantric Buddhism, Tibetan Lamaism, Chinese and Japanese "Pure Land" Buddhism, Zen, and others. Famous Mahayana sutras, such as the Lotus sutra and the Heart sutra, were composed hundreds of years after the death of Gautama, but Mahayana Buddhism embraces the idea that the dharma is a "higher truth" than mere historical chronology. In fact, many Mahayana sutras claim to be the result of a divine transmission, coming not from the mortal Gautama, but from some transhistorical immortal manifestation. Other Mahayana schools eschew the "divine transmission" thesis and just accept the idea that the dharma is a living, evolving tradition.

The earlier school of Theravada tended to stress the historical Gautama and his teachings (the Tripitika scriptures), while the Mahayana schools tended to see Gautama as just one "chapter" in a larger "book" of dharma wisdom, with additional chapters being transmitted during later historical eras.

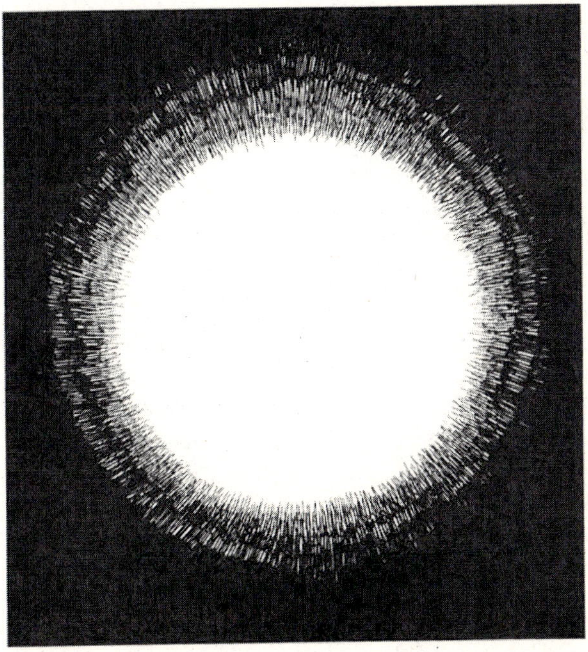

Even in some of the earliest texts, the historical Buddha began to be characterized as "more than" a human being. Mystical embellishments, some quite recognizable to Westerners (e.g., virgin birth, devilish temptations, miraculous cures, and so on) became attached to Gautama's life. Buddhism, like most religions, had two dimensions: a popular ideology for the majority of devotees, and a more sophisticated set of doctrines and issues for the scholars and monks. The more popular version tended to interpret the Buddha as a deity. Stories multiplied, for example, about his superpowers and his adventures in other worlds and previous lives.

Both during his own lifetime and after his death, questions regarding the uniqueness of the Buddha became important. How could such a great teacher be a mere human being? Will the Enlightened One pass from this mortal coil to a transcendental heaven after death? Is the Buddha a god in disguise?

Nagarjuna, who began the Madhyamika sect in the second century CE, was probably the most influential philosopher of the Mahayana school. He developed his philosophy by focusing on those questions that Gautama had refused to answer. When asked whether the enlightened person exists or not after death, the Buddha enigmatically responded by denying the four possible options: the enlightened one does exist, the enlightened one does not exist, the enlightened one both does and does not exist, and the enlightened one neither exists nor does not exist.

From the fact that the Buddha rejected all these responses, Nagarjuna argued that language (and any method by which we try to represent reality) is unable to grasp the inexpressible infinite truth behind our limited experience. The Buddha, according to Nagarjuna, was purposely responding paradoxically in order to convey this deeper reality, the unspeakable Absolute. Like the Western theologians who argue that God's infinite nature is inexpressible and dimly understood by our finite natures, Nagarjuna argues that ultimate reality is ineffable or unsayable. Instead of calling this fundamental reality "God" and attributing personality traits to it, Nagarjuna refers to it as "emptiness" or "void" (sunya) to indicate its inexpressible character.

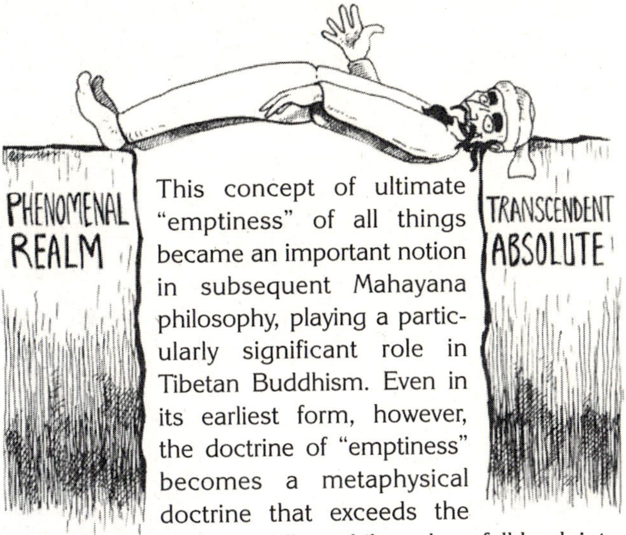

This concept of ultimate "emptiness" of all things became an important notion in subsequent Mahayana philosophy, playing a particularly significant role in Tibetan Buddhism. Even in its earliest form, however, the doctrine of "emptiness" becomes a metaphysical doctrine that exceeds the teachings of Gautama. Some Buddhist philosophers fell back into the earlier Hindu metaphysics of "two worlds": one, the day-to-day physical world of our experience; and two, the transcendental unspeakable Absolute (or emptiness). The bridge between these worlds, they argued, was the Buddha himself, an incarnation of the transcendental Absolute that we finite humans could relate to in some fashion.

Of course, this sounds very similar to the Christian concept of an earthly and a heavenly realm with Jesus as a mediating go-between. In Christian theology, however, God reaches down to the human realm, but in this strain of Buddhism, a human reaches up to a nonpersonal transcendent Absolute. But no matter what banner it parades under, this two-world metaphysics is not Buddhism.

The real purpose of Buddhist talk about "emptiness" is not to postulate some other realm, but to remind us of the radical impermanence of all things. Seen in that light, the emptiness of all things is just another, albeit more extreme, way of saying there is no permanent soul (anatman) and no permanent Brahman (pratitya samutpada).

Given the corruption of some Buddhism into a form of dualism, it is easy to see how "nirvana" could be misconstrued as a kind of heaven. Lay Buddhism, in the larger popular culture, especially fell prey to this confusion. Meanwhile, Buddhist philosophers of four major schools (Sarvastivadins, Sautrantikas, Madhyamikas, and Yogacarins) fell on themselves, arguing over just how empty the emptiness really was.

Some Mahayana sects continued this deification of Gautama, but, as they did so, other characters began to populate their pantheon. That is to say, for some Mahayana Buddhists, particularly in popular Buddhism, there is not just one avatar, there are many. The historical Buddha repeatedly claimed that his elevated state of enlightenment was available to others, and that he was not utterly unique from other awakened ones (arhats or tathagatas). This emphasis forces the devotee to avoid idolatry of the medium, and focus instead upon the message. Mahayana Buddhism transforms this notion into the belief in Bodhisattvas (fledgling Buddhas, as it were).

The idea of the Bodhisattva is an interesting development in the history of Buddhist philosophy because it reorients the devotee away from the individualistic goal of self-awakening towards the more socially responsible activity of helping others to gain new ground in the struggle. A Bodhisattva is a person who has liberated herself to the extent that she could pass into nirvana, but chooses to stay in the world of suffering (samsara) in order to teach and aid others in the quest for freedom. Early descriptions of Bodhisattvas (e.g., the Prajnaparamita text) characterized them as human beings that had risen to a new level through their selfless, compassionate devotion to others. This seems like a healthy amendment to the radical individualism of the early Buddhist ideal—the lone searcher striving for and winning nirvana for himself only.

An unfortunate by-product of these amendments to early Buddhism is that these new spiritual teachers also went the way of Gautama's image, quickly degenerating into mythic idols for reverential worship. Buddhism developed a pantheon of divinities—deities to be intoned in times of trouble, to be sacrificed to, to be prostrated before, and to be bribed. Bodhisattvas, Buddhas, and various other saints increasingly became supernatural beings and as such increasingly distracted the average person from the business of freedom. In short, certain forms of Buddhism evolved into the very mistakes that Gautama fought against in Hinduism.

One of the forms most divergent from Gautama's teachings is probably the "Tantric" or magical sect of Buddhism. This form developed around the sixth or seventh century CE and it spread most notably to Tibet where it had a major influence. Tantric Buddhism further accentuates the trend, which began in the Mahayana schools, of separating average ordinary devotees from a rising class of supposed "gnostics" (an elite of people who are "in the know" regarding spiritual matters). The Tantric sect widens the gap between teacher and student until it becomes like a parent-child relationship of guru to pupil. Once the Tantric school divides people into camps of initiated and uninitiated, it quickly makes spiritual success dependent on one's subservience to a guru. This hierarchy is a distinct break from Gautama's message of equal-access freedom. Much of the historical Buddha's disgust with the caste system stems from his view that each human independently has the ability and the responsibility to perfect him or herself. Teachers are good; guru "masters" are suspicious.

Another aspect of Tantric thought that seems to run counter to early Buddhism is its strong emphasis upon magic. Mantra is Sanskrit for "spell" and Tantric Buddhism encouraged the practice of casting spells to protect oneself and generally influence the cosmos in one's favor. Chanting a phrase over and over has become a fairly significant aspect of some Buddhist schools, but it has little to do with original Buddhism. In addition to the practice of casting spells and dabbling in the occasional hex, the Tantric school engages in excruciatingly elaborate rituals. Complicated prayers and the sprinkling of holy water, for example, are aspects of some Tantric initiation rites.

There are two important reasons why this later development is not in step with, and may be quite inconsistent with, the historical Buddha's teachings. First, it seems rather unlikely that Gautama would agree to populate the cosmos with mystical forces when he would not even agree to acknowledge his own soul. He showed himself to be hostile towards our strong tendency to postulate hidden agencies (most important, atman) where none could be confirmed. And the existence or nonexistence of occult spirits has exactly no bearing whatsoever on the task of enlightenment. As the Buddha suggests, regarding a similarly insignificant metaphysical issue, there is no consequence to these matters because "there is still rebirth, there is old age, there is death, and grief, lamentation, suffering, sorrow and despair, the destruction of which even in this life I announce" (Majjhima Nikaya, chapter 11).

The second reason why the magical elements of later Buddhism seem contrary to Gautama's teachings is that they run counter to the laws of causality. According to early Buddhism, no amount of prayers, spells, or ritual practices can reverse or mitigate the inexorable law of karma. Influencing the future is not done with prayerful entreaties or superstitious ceremonies; it is accomplished via the causal law by moral action. The practice of magical ceremonies designed to manipulate events presupposes the decidedly non-Buddhist attitude that we are pawns in a fortuitous cosmic game. Through mystical rites one vainly hopes to negotiate with the causal law. But according to Gautama, there is only one way of perfecting oneself and eventually escaping the wheel of becoming, and it is accomplished through the annihilation of craving via the Eightfold Path.

Another important development in the history of Buddhism is the sect devoted to the supernatural Buddha named Amitabha. Amitabha, the Buddha of Infinite Light, is a divine being who lives in a heavenly paradise. This school's major text source is the Sukhavati sutra, which describes this blissful promised land for devotees. Though originating in northern India, the sect made great strides in China after the seventh century CE and Japan after the tenth century CE. In Japan, the school evolved into the "True Sect of the Pure Land" and continues to dominate Japanese Buddhism.

The sect's tremendous popularity is undoubtedly related to its simple and undemanding doctrine. Believe in Amitabha, and go to heaven; disbelieve, and you won't. No tortuous theology here, no rigorous yoga, no struggle for moral perfection.

According to some Pure Land sects, anyone who has faith (regardless of that person's moral worth or social status) can be a Buddhist in good standing. Of course the "egalitarian" character of this sect is in tune with the historical Buddha's teachings, but just about everything else in the Pure Land school is rather discordant. "Faith" is not only uninteresting in early Buddhism, it is unintelligible. Unless one means by "faith" a belief in the efficacy of the Eightfold Path (and the Pure Land sect means significantly more by it), then it is hard to envision its meaning for Buddhism. After all, there are no gods to have faith in, no rituals to blindly trust, no objects to venerate, no dogma to which to commit. For the historical Buddha, there is only Right Action and Right Understanding.

Faith has also come to play a major role in the popular American school of Buddhism, Soka Gakkai. By repeatedly chanting the mantra "nam-myoho-renge-kyo" ("praise to the mystic law of the Lotus sutra"), the devotees endeavor to transform themselves and their world into a happier place. But over the centuries, chanting, magic, and mysticism have grown on top of Buddhism like a thick kudzu vine, making it hard to see the real dharma underneath. For Gautama, we cannot control the external world by faith in magical mantras, so we must learn to control our minds by psychological discipline.

One last school worth touching upon is perhaps the most widely recognized in the United States, namely Zen Buddhism. "Zen" (Chinese ch'an) means "meditation," and this Mahayana school took its lead from the Buddha's practice of contemplation. Zen seems to have begun in the seventh century CE in China and spread to Japan in the thirteenth century.

While it was in China, the movement certainly incorporated significant aspects of Taoism, one of the indigenous philosophies that emphasized harmony with nature. Zen adopts the Taoist idea that the "way" (tao) of effortless harmony is a meditative attitude that can transform daily activities (like drinking tea) into spiritual exercises.

There is also an emphasis, particularly in the Rinzai subsect of Zen, upon the contemplation of irrational puzzles called "koans." One of the favorite koans, well known to many Westerners, is the question: "What is the sound of one hand clapping?" These riddles have an interesting connection with the earlier Mahayana philosophies of the Yogacarins. Both schools emphasized the act of meditation (quiet reflection or struggle with paradoxes) as a means of breaking down the ordinary concepts by which we organize our experience and letting our minds intuit the Ideal Reality. When the devotee escapes from thinking in terms of subjects and objects—dividing the world into artificial categories—she may achieve "satori" (sudden illumination) and this is a major step towards full enlightenment.

Most Zen schools are similar to early Buddhism in their rejection of tradition and scripture. By focusing on mundane actions, we can attune ourselves to the elusive present moment (the truest reality in our impermanent world). The idea of Zen practice is to clear away all of the distractions of dogma and focus inwardly upon a detached awareness of the present moment. Some schools, however, foster a strong dependence on a guru (roshi) for spiritual progress, and this has the potential to degenerate into another Buddhist hierarchy.

Clearly, Buddhism has undergone incredible changes since the time of Gautama. For two and a half millennia, Buddhism has been an evolving mosiac of ideas and practices.

By the thirteenth century CE, however, Buddhism ceased to play an important role in India, having been both driven out by Muslim invaders and assimilated back into Hinduism.

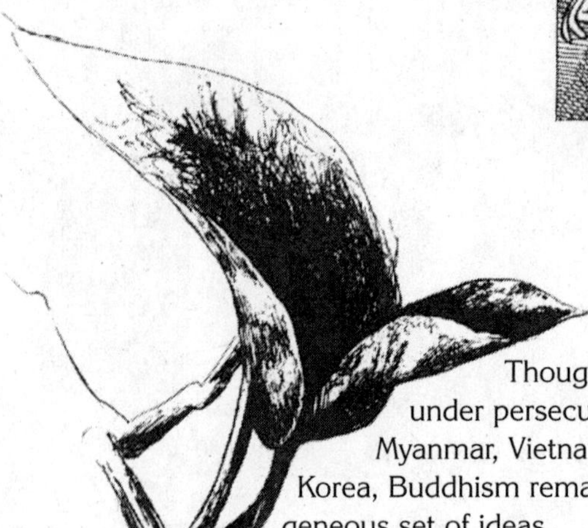

Though it continues to fall under persecution in nations such as Myanmar, Vietnam, Tibet, and North Korea, Buddhism remains a powerful if heterogeneous set of ideas.

One final issue in the philosophy and history of Buddhism needs to be examined. The role of women, both in early and later Buddhism, is an interesting story. Some have suggested that, when compared to other world religions, women fare pretty well in Buddhism. Indeed, there is much in the egalitarian tone of early Buddhist scriptures to suggest an enlightened view of women. Moreover, the early legends surrounding Gautama's life claim that he returned to his family after enlightenment and founded the first order of nuns, having been inspired by the wisdom of his Aunt Prajapati (stepmother).

In a rather bold break from tradition, the Buddha argued that women are equally capable as men of mastering their cravings and ultimately becoming enlightened ones. A monastic order of nuns was initiated and apparently thrived in India from the time of the Buddha until the third or fourth century CE, after which it diminished drastically. The fate of women in Buddhism was foreshadowed in the earliest texts by confused and contradictory images, and the vacillating importance of asceticism.

We have already seen that Gautama's attitude towards asceticism is more sophisticated than the draconian measures of contemporaries such as the Jains. Recall his argument that pleasures of the flesh were not inherently wicked. Instead, it was the turmoil of desire that could arise in the wake of pleasure that Gautama sought to destroy. Theoretically, one can affect this destruction even while experiencing pleasure. Nonetheless, the earliest monasteries, or groups of devotees, were to live according to a strict code of conduct called "the Rule." This Rule, which some attribute to Gautama himself, attempted to create an environment with little or no temptations to distract the devotee. Lust between the sexes was considered just another catalyst for craving, and every attempt was made in the monastic movements that followed Gautama's death to avoid this particularly strident bodily temptation.

The historical Buddha may have contributed to the ambivalence towards women by championing their right to, and capability for, "renunciation" on the one hand, but characterizing them in the Dhammapada (and other texts) as falling high on the list of things for monks to carefully avoid. Monks who were seeking to avoid the temptations of the sensual world demonized women into the symbols of all things earthly. Women seem to get this same rap wherever patriarchal structures mix with asceticism, in both Eastern and Western religions.

It is important to note, however, that it is only in the monastic Buddhist traditions (which quickly became male-dominant through preferential patronage) that this misogynist trend flourished. Unfortunately, the optimistic start that Gautama made by recognizing "female buddha-hood" was ultimately undone when Buddhism slowly melted back into the larger Hindu culture (Buddha was just recast as an incarnation of a Hindu god). The Hindu emphasis on social order, and individual conformity to that order, led the culture to look with deep suspicion and hostility upon a woman who was neither a wife nor a mother. Women following the asocial path of enlightenment were increasingly alone and without the needed support of the populace.

Some forms of the Tantric school (for all its other corruptions of early Buddhism) do seem to have taken a far healthier attitude towards the body, towards sexuality, and towards women than most other forms of Buddhism. Some Tantric mystic sects, probably drawing upon early Dravidian cultural influences, celebrate the female as a powerful cosmic principle. Male and female deities derive their mystical energies through sexuality, according to this theology, so why not us humans? Subsequently, sexuality actually becomes a vehicle for salvation, and gender relations take on a less bigoted tone.

'NUFF SAID.

Postscript

To examine the complex debates of early and later Buddhism is an eye-opening experience. For some time now, the West has been stereotyping the East as a convenient "other," a land of intuition and enigma. Philosophical traditions such as Buddhism are seen as deeply irrational, inherently mysterious, and ultimately inscrutable. Lamentably, this stereotype has been used by those rationalist Westerners who hope to feel superior to the "backward" Eastern people. But more recently, the same stereotype is being employed by "New Age" Westerners to elevate irrationalism and mysticism, claiming Eastern intuitionism as the righteous path out of Western exploitation and alienation. One group shouts out Buddhism's difference from Western philosophy with derision in their voices, and the other group shouts out Buddhism's difference with adoration in their voices.

The irony of all this is that when one actually digs beneath the piles of self-improvement styled, pop-spiritual dreck to find the original source material of both traditions, an astounding solidarity of common questions and methods emerges. Aristotle and the early Hinayana philosophers, for example, struggle with very similar questions of permanence and change in quite analogous ways. Or compare Gautama's and the Stoic Epictetus's moral philosophy, in which a similar self-mastery of the passions becomes the highest freedom in a world of servitude. In short, anybody who thinks that Buddhists are less rational than Westerners should read their Nagarjuna. And anybody who thinks that Westerners are narrowly logistic should read their Plato.

Some Further Reading

PRIMARY SOURCES

Buddhism in Practice, edited by Donald S. Lopez Jr. (Princeton University Press, 2007).

A Buddhist Bible, edited by Dwight Goddard (Beacon Press, 1994).

Buddhist Wisdom: Containing the Diamond Sutra and the Heart Sutra, translated and explained by Edward Conze (Vintage Books, 2001).

A Comprehensive Manual of Abhidhamma, edited by Bhikkhu Bodhi (Pariyatti Publishing, 2000).

The Connected Discourses of the Buddha: A New Translation of the Samyutta Nikaya, original translation by Bhikkhu Bodhi (Wisdom Publications, 2000).

The Fundamental Wisdom of the Middle Way, Nagarjuna's Mulamadhyamakakarika, translation and commentary by Jay L. Garfield (Oxford University Press, 1995).

The Long Discourses of the Buddha: A Translation of the Digha Nikaya, translated from the Pali by Maurice Walshe (Wisdom Publications, 1995).

The Middle Length Discourses of the Buddha: A New Translation of the Majjhima Nikaya, translated, edited, and revised by Bhikkhu Bodhi (Wisdom Publications, 1995).

The Perfection of Wisdom (Prajnaparamita), translated by Edward Conze (Grey Fox Press, 1989).

A Source Book in Indian Philosophy, edited by Sarvepalli Radhakrishnan and Charles A. Moore (Princeton University Press, 1967).

SECONDARY SOURCES

Buddha, Marx, and God: Some Aspects of Religion in the Modern World, by Trevor Ling (St. Martin's Press, 1966).

Buddhism: Its Essence and Development, by Edward Conze (Harper & Bros., 1959).

Buddhism Plain and Simple, by Steve Hagen (Broadway Books, 1999).

Buddhists, Brahmins, and Belief: Epistemology in South Asian Philosophy of Religion, by Daniel Anderson Arnold (Columbia University Press, 2005).

Cambodian Buddhism: History and Practice, by Ian Harris (University of Hawaii Press, 2005).

Causality: The Central Philosophy of Buddhism, by David J. Kalupahana (University Press of Hawaii, 1975).

A Concise History of Buddhism, by Andrew Skilton (Barnes & Noble, 1994).

The Dalai Lama at Harvard: Lectures on the Buddhist Path to Peace, by His Holiness the Dalai Lama, translated and edited by Jeffrey Hopkins (Snow Lion Publications, 1988).

Engaged Buddhism: Buddhist Liberation Movements in Asia, edited by Christopher S. Queen and Sallie B. King (State University of New York Press, 1996).

Heartwood of the Bodhi Tree: The Buddha's Teachings on Voidness, by Buddhadasa Bhikkhu (Wisdom Publications, 1994).

Nagarjuna: The Philosophy of the Middle Way, by David J. Kalupahana (State University of New York Press, 1986).

Theravada Buddhism: A Social History from Ancient Benares to Colombo, by Richard F. Gombrich (Routledge & Kegan Paul, 1988).

What the Buddha Taught, by Walpola Rahula (Grove Press, 1974).

Women in Buddhism: Images of the Feminine in Mahayana Tradition, by Diana Y. Paul (University of California Press, 1985).

Women under Primitive Buddhism: Laywomen and Almswomen, by I. B. Horner (G. Routledge & Sons, 1930).

Index

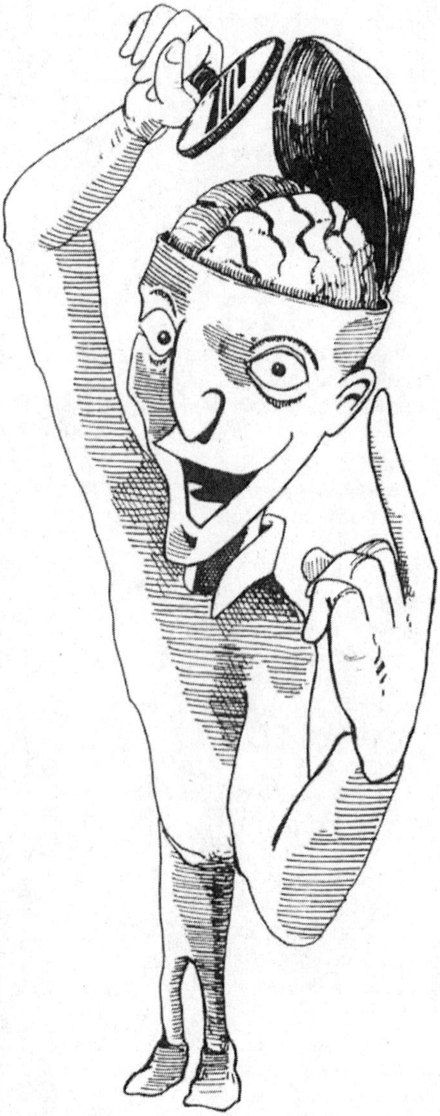

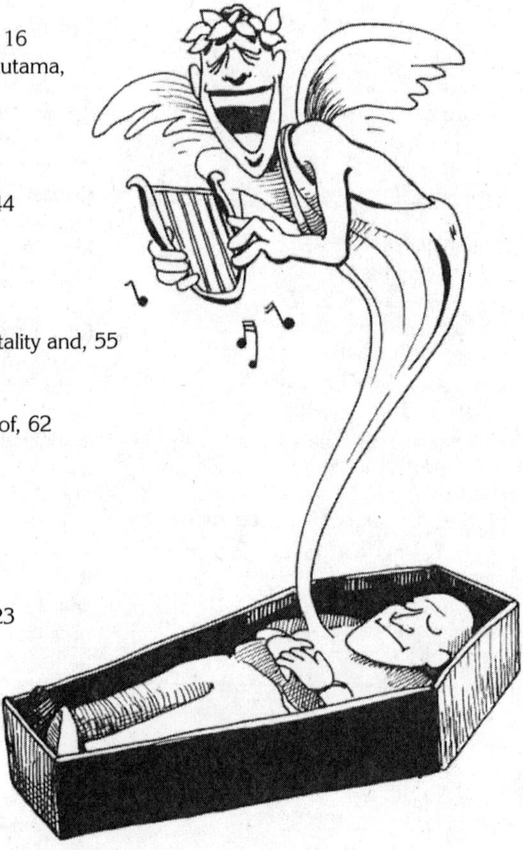

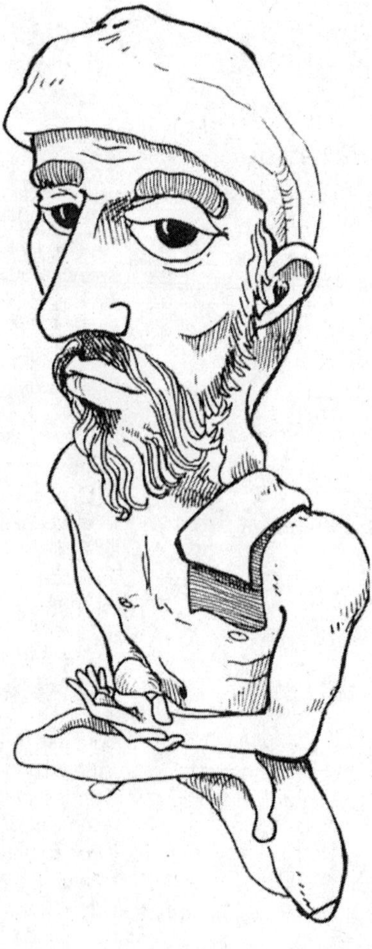

About the Author

Stephen T. Asma, PhD, is professor of philosophy at Columbia College Chicago, where he holds the title of Distinguished Scholar.

In 2003, he was visiting professor at the Buddhist Institute in Phnom Penh, Kingdom of Cambodia. There he taught "Buddhist Philosophy" as part of their pilot graduate program in Buddhist studies, and he studied Theravada Buddhism throughout Southeast Asia. His book entitled The Gods Drink Whiskey: Stumbling toward Enlightenment in the Land of the Tattered Buddha chronicles his adventures in Asia. He has also lived and studied Buddhism in Shanghai, China.

Dr. Asma's other books include Stuffed Animals and Pickled Heads: The Culture and Evolution of Natural History Museums and the forthcoming Why I Am a Buddhist. He has written many articles on a broad range of topics that bridge the humanities, religion, and sciences, including "Against Transcendentalism" in the book Monty Python and Philosophy and "Dinosaurs on the Ark: Natural History and the New Creation Museum" in The Chronicle of Higher Education. He has also written for the Chicago Tribune and Skeptic magazine. Dr. Asma has been a guest lecturer at many institutions, including Harvard's Museum of Comparative Zoology and Chicago's Field Museum, and he is regularly invited to give dharma talks at Buddhist temples.